FREE Stuff & Good Deals for Folks over 50

by Linda Bowman

3rd Edition

SANTA MONICA PRESS

SANTA

MONICA

PRESS

Published by:
Santa Monica Press LLC
P.O. Box 1076
Santa Monica, CA 90406-1076
1-800-784-9553
www.santamonicapress.com

Printed in the United States

Santa Monica Press books are available at special quantity discounts when purchased in bulk by corporations, organizations, or groups. Please call our Special Sales department at 1-800-784-9553.

This book is intended to provide general information. The publisher, author, distributor, and copyright owner are not engaged in rendering health, medical, legal, financial, or other professional advice or services. Be aware that offers, phone numbers, addresses, web sites, etc. may have changed. The publisher, author, distributor, and copyright owner are not liable or responsible to any person or group with respect to any loss, illness, or injury caused or alleged to be caused by the information found in this book.

ISBN-13 978-1-59580-027-5
ISBN-10 1-59580-027-1

Library of Congress Cataloging-in-Publication Data

Bowman, Linda.
Free stuff & good deals for folks over 50 / by Linda Bowman. — 3rd ed.
    p. cm.
    ISBN 978-1-59580-027-5
1. Discounts for older people—United States. 2. Older people—Services for--United States. 3. Older people—Recreation—United States. 4. Older people—Travel—United States. I. Title. II. Title: Free stuff and good deals for folks over 50.

HQ1064.U5B685 2008
362.60973--dc22

2007041435

Book and cover design by Lynda "Cool Dog" Jakovich

Illustrations by Jorge Pacheco

Contents

CHAPTER 3

CHAPTER 4

CHAPTER 5

Have the Time of Your Life in the Prime of Your Life

This book is for those of us who know we are on the threshold of what should and can be the very best years of our lives. There are nearly 70 million Americans over the age of 50. We are as varied, active, interesting, vital and exciting as any group can be. However, as a group, there are only two things we have in common:

1. We were born more than 50 years ago; and
2. We have earned admittance into the incredible, wonderful, wide world of "freebies" and special discounts for folks over 50.

Because of the variety of our interests, abilities, and activities, and the differences between segments within the 50+ age group, there is no name or label that properly identifies everyone. The new definition of "middle age" has been set as the years between 44 and 66. With that being the case, forget the idea of "senior." Most of us between these ages are enjoying the "prime of our life," i.e. middle age. For the sake of simplifying terms, I will use "mature adult" and "senior citizen" interchangeably throughout this book, hopefully satisfying the majority of my readers, whether you have just turned 50 or are nearing 90. Since more mature adults claim to feel, on the average, 15 years younger than their chronological age, labels have become nearly meaningless.

Along with the problem of labeling folks 50 and over, are the false assumptions and stereotypes that sometimes accompany those labels:

- Mature adults are all the same;
- Mature adults are always becoming ill and suffer from poor health;
- Mature adults have nothing to contribute to society;
- Mature adults are set in their ways, stubborn, and difficult;
- Mature adults are draining our country of its funds;
- Mature adults are weak and non-influential;
- Mature adults should be retired at age 65;
- Mature adults are poorer than other segments of the population;
- Mature adults are basically lonely;
- Mature adults lose their mental faculties and can't think or reason as well as they used to;
- Mature adults prefer the company of older people like themselves;
- Mature adults are physically inactive and become more sedentary as they get older.

I could go on, but be aware that all of the above statements and any others you've heard are entirely false, foolish and without substance. In fact, in every case the reverse is true:

- You can be healthier, happier, and live longer now than ever before;
- Your financial situation can be significantly better and continue to improve after you reach 50;
- Your relationships and friendships can be deeper and more meaningful than before. Romance can even get better with experience, time, and maturity on your side;
- Your health can remain excellent and you can participate in nearly any physical activity you choose;
- Your mental faculties can be sharper, your senses keener, and your beliefs and needs more focused than they were in your youth;
- Your choices are greater than ever, with more time on your hands and the freedom to do what you want whenever you want;
- You can achieve goals you've always aspired to, rising to new levels of knowledge and ability. Learning and becoming are processes that live as long as you do;
- You can make an important difference in the quality of your life and the lives of all mature adults;
- You alone have the ability and wisdom to cross generational barriers and communicate, teach, and reach out to others of all ages.

Mature adults are the fastest growing segment of the population, representing nearly a quarter of the people in the United States today. As a result, the business community is intensely aware of the purchasing power held by mature adults. With over $1 billion in combined annual income and $300 million in discretionary income, seniors as consumers are a formidable force. In addition, the dozens of senior organizations, associations and advocacy groups representing millions of people over the age of 50 are no longer ignored by our leaders and lawmakers on Capitol Hill. Meeting the growing needs and demands of this group will continue to be a significant challenge in the future.

Products and services that focus on the mature market with freebies, discounts and privileges continue to grow yearly as the number of seniors continues to increase. Some of the areas offering freebies, discounts and great deals that I discuss in this book include:

- Transportation: airlines, car rentals, trains, buses;
- Entertainment: concerts, movies, theater, attractions, theme parks, restaurants, sports events, fairs, museums, zoos, aquariums, historical sites;
- Sports: Senior Olympic and multi-sport competitions, tennis, golf, swimming, walking, skiing, cross-country skiing, dancing, running, biking, bowling;
- Shopping: chain department stores, bookstores, toy stores, home repair services, automobile repair services, gasoline service stations;
- Travel: cruises, tours, travel clubs, hotels, motels, resorts, free travel, adventure travel, package

deals, national parks and recreation areas, travel with grandchildren;

- Financial Investments, Savings and Insurance: bank and S&L discounts and perks, retirement and investment advice, free insurance information, tax advice;
- Education: travel/study programs, free and low-cost adult education programs, college and university programs, computer networking for seniors;
- Health: health screenings, medical and dental services, free information, treatment, preventative programs, medicine, and prescription drugs.

These topics include some of the major areas of interest to mature adults. In addition I've included some helpful suggestions and guidelines to aid you in getting these deals and enjoying them as much as possible.

There are some terrific opportunities out there waiting for mature adults. Freebies and savings can be found nearly everywhere. Not only can you save when you're having fun (which is where most people think all the savings are), but you can save at the bank, where you shop, going back to school, and in your health care needs. You can save from $1 to thousands of dollars, from 10% to 90% by being aware and informed of the hundreds of special senior privileges, discounts, and perks available just because you've turned 50. Some of the freebies and deals that I've included are available to all age groups—not just seniors. I just want to make sure you are aware of them.

Ask and You Shall Receive

To take advantage of these deals, all you need to do is ask for them. The two most important questions to ask are:

- "Do you have discounts for seniors?"
- "What is the lowest available rate?"

Memorize these questions and use them everywhere you go to purchase products and services: at restaurants, movies, booking travel arrangements, theater events, sporting events, at the cleaners, at your bank . . . anywhere and everywhere. Soon you will be realizing savings you never thought possible. And they weren't, before now. You have entered a new life and a new world. They say life is a series of passages. Today, being 50 and older means passing through the wide doors of enjoying the best things in life. So why not enjoy them for less and even for free?

Serious Shopping and Savings

Mature adults are a loyal group when it comes to shopping and choosing products and services. Smart retailers and companies in the business of serving the public know that mature people want quality and service they can depend on, and will reward those who satisfy their needs by coming back again and again.

The American Association for Retired Persons, commonly known as AARP, also provides a wealth of discount programs for those over the age of 50. More detailed information on AARP and other associations and organizations that offer benefits for senior adults can be found in Chapter 7 of this book.

Major chain stores that offer senior citizen discounts include:
- Barnes & Noble www.barnesandnoble.com. More than 1,000 stores throughout the country. Their Member Program entitles members to a 10 percent discount on all books and accessories (including items on sale), a 20 percent discount on adult hardcovers, and a 40 percent discount on hardcover bestsellers. There is an annual $25.00 membership fee to join.
- Kohl's Department stores offer senior discounts on special days in December, and several times throughout the year. Ask at your local Kohl's.
- Ross Clothing Stores offer a 10 percent discount to those over 55 every Tuesday.
- Sally Beauty Supply offers discounts of 5 percent to 25 percent to seniors 55 and older.

Senior citizen newspapers often carry advertising by local establishments for discounts of at least 10 percent. Some discounts are good only on certain days of the week or are offered on a "limited time only" basis. In most cases you need to ask for the discount at the time of purchase or service. Here are some recent examples of discounts:
- 10 percent off toys, games, and hobbies at a regional chain of toy stores.
- 15 percent on any purchase, regular or sale, for one day at a popular chain department store.

- Senior citizen discount coupons available from a local taxi company.
- Senior citizen discounts from a distributor of medical, burglary, and fire alarms and security systems.
- 10 percent senior citizen discount for all automotive service repairs from a tire and brake service garage.
- 10 percent discount to seniors over 50 on all orders from a collectibles mail order catalog.
- Senior citizen coupon worth $1 off the cost of a car wash.
- 10 percent senior citizen discount on television repair service.
- 10 percent senior citizen discount on window washing.
- 10 percent senior citizen discount on veterinarian services.
- 20 percent senior citizen discount on medical services of a general practitioner.
- 15 to 25 percent senior citizen discount on dental services.
- 15 percent senior citizen discount on the services of an electrician and 10 percent off the cost of services of a handyman.
- Senior discount offered on house painting, carpentry, and concrete and block work.
- 41 percent senior citizen discount on regular price acrylic yarn from super yarn mart.

If you want to take advantage of self-service prices at gas stations, but have a problem doing it yourself (pumping gas can be hard on stiff joints and limbs), individual station owners are often sympathetic to the less agile older citizen's plight. Speak with the manager or owner about arranging a time to come in for gas when business is usually slow. They may help you fill up at the self-service tank when they are not busy with other customers. Avoid gas station-convenience store combos or high-volume gas stations. Some operate with only one or two cashiers who are unable to leave their posts to help customers.

State senior citizen discount programs include businesses offering senior discounts (in addition to the discounts seniors receive at state parks, campgrounds, fishing areas, historic sites, etc.). A member of the program can use his or her membership card to obtain discounts at establishments participating in the senior discount program. In California, participants advertising in the Yellow Pages of the phone directory display a special symbol in their ads to notify consumers that they belong to the program. Check with your state's Office/Department on Aging for a list of businesses in the senior citizen discount program.

Remember the Internet!

Just a few years ago, the Internet was something only "techies" understood. It was a strange world located in the foreign galaxy of cyberspace that was off limits to all but the most computer-savvy folks. What a difference a few years can make!

Today, I *highly* recommend you learn to use the "net" and "surf" your way to the knowledge and savings that are just a mouse click away. Nearly every commercial and consumer entity now has a web site, and navigation around cyberspace is becoming easier all the time. Millions of seniors are discovering the cyber world—a place to connect with far-flung family and friends through e-mail, sharing grandchildren's photos and so much more. As many as 2 million folks regularly visit www.cyberseniors.org, a site devoted to creating a virtual online community and empowering seniors with Internet skills. It features basic tips for cyber rookies and valuable links to health, hobby, and lifestyle sites, including fun sites that offer recipes and candy factory tours. (The site also offers in-person workshops around the country to teach seniors how to use the Internet). The Internet provides a powerful and fun lifeline for active seniors as well as shut-ins.

If you don't have your own computer, you can use one for free at your local library. If the idea of the Internet is confusing and overwhelming to you, check with your local high school, senior center or adult learning center for free or low-cost courses in using this amazing technological tool. Or, better yet, ask one of your family members or colleagues at work if they would be willing to give you some lessons. Most people, especially adult children and grandchildren are happy to teach you their online skills. This is a great opportunity to bond with a co-worker or younger family member who, in turn, will get the satisfaction of teaching you something that can enhance your life. In addition to www.cyberseniors.org, you can also jump right in, dial up the Internet, and go to "50+ Web Guide" at www.smartandrich.com. Once you've learned the basics, you will quickly catch on to the shortcuts and tricks of finding nearly anything and everything you desire.

Another web site, www.seniornet.org, offers regular discussion groups and member blogs, where users can "talk" about various topics. www.seniornet.org has lots of information on Internet basics, along with bulletin boards where one can post comments and replies on various topics, including gardening, music, politics and health. Check out www.seniors-site.com which features an array of message boards for general discussions as well as those focused on health and legal issues. An "Ask an Expert" feature allows visitors to e-mail questions to authorities on care giving, grandparenting, computers and more.

I have included many web sites, in addition to phone numbers and addresses, to make your search for savings and freebies as easy as possible. To accommodate the swelling online ranks of older Americans, web sites devoted solely to seniors have sprouted up, providing a wealth of resources targeted at the over-50 crowd, with chat rooms and message boards that bring seniors together over a wide range of topics. Surfing the world and socializing from the comfort of an armchair is convenient for anyone, but understandably holds a special appeal for many seniors. E-mail is usually the main reason seniors decide to go online. Then you can jump in and explore health resources and even make new friends. As you get more comfortable navigating the Internet, you can begin using this invaluable source for tracking finances, doing banking and making purchases. I encourage you to explore these sites, which, in many cases, will lead you to additional sites and links to help you find exactly what you need.

Welcome to the world of senior savings and have the time of your life in the prime of your life!!

CHAPTER 1

Let Us Entertain You (for Less!)

One of the most exciting and diverse areas for great senior deals and discounts is the area of entertainment. Wherever you go to have a good time and enjoy yourself, you can probably do it for less than the price listed, and sometimes even for free. Some of these attractions and entertainment opportunities include: Movies, dances, company tours, concerts, theme parks, museums, historical sites, theaters, restaurants, tourist attractions, and sporting events.

Always ask about a senior citizen discount before buying a ticket or paying an entrance fee. It's not always advertised that such discounts are available. You should always carry your driver's license (or other proof of age I.D.) or membership card in an over-50 club as proof that you deserve a break. A lot of folks who have kept fit and healthy simply don't look 50 or 55 and may be asked for proof of age. Remember when they used to "card" you when you needed to be 21 to get into a club or other "adult" venue? Here you are again, being asked, "Are you sure you're 50? You don't look it."

Movies and Concerts

Free movies and concerts are some of the most enjoyable events offered nearly everywhere, often on a weekly or monthly basis at the same location. Senior centers, libraries, museums, and public auditoriums make use of their empty spaces and community rooms during the day by running classic movies, educational movies, or special movie series.

There are also free daytime concerts given by musical groups who volunteer their talents in the community. For example, summer concert series and holiday musical performances in shopping centers and malls. Parks and recreation departments also sponsor free events (often aimed at retirees and those who are free from daily jobs and family obligations) such as dances and concerts given by local school bands, dance and music departments. Many of the performers themselves are retired professionals or working professionals who still perform regularly at "paying" events. These concerts give those who can't afford the steep price of tickets a chance to experience quality musical events.

For example, the following free events were recently listed in my local metropolitan newspaper:

- George Coleman and the Harold Mabern Quartet kick off the "Summer Nights At MOCA" weekly summer series featuring jazz and blues performances, wine and beer tastings and gallery tours at the Museum of Contemporary Art. 5–8 P.M. Free music every Thursday.
- The Playboy Jazz Festival presents "Jazz on Film," a two-hour compilation of film clips featuring classic performances by Charlie Parker, Dexter

Gordon, Billie Holiday, Chet Baker, Dinah Washington, Willie "The Lion" Smith, and others, at the Los Angeles County Museum of Art. 7:30 P.M. Admission is free.

- Trumpeter Jeff Beal's combo performs with pianist Alan Pasqua at the Los Angeles County Museum of Art, 5:50–8:30 P.M.
- "Music Under the Stars" features the Pasadena Pops Orchestra and the Gospel Choirs of First A.M.E Church of Los Angeles performing music by Leonard Bernstein, Tchalkovsky, and others, outdoors at Pasadena City Hall, 7:30 P.M.
- Laura Krafft hosts the comedy variety show "The Extravaganza at ImprovOlympic West," 9 P.M.

During the summer months weekly free music is performed at the following venues:

- Autry National Center, Griffith Park, 6:30–9 P.M. Thursdays;
- Santa Monica Pier, 7:30–9:30 P.M. Thursdays;
- Skirball Cultural Center, 8 P.M. Thursdays;
- Los Angeles County Museum of Art, 6–8 P.M., Fridays;
- UCLA Hammer Museum, 8 P.M. Thursdays;
- California Plaza, Downtown LA, noon and 8 P.M. Fridays and Saturdays.

Additionally, you can nearly always save money off the adult ticket price at first-run movies. Discounts run from 25–75% off regular ticket prices. With the price of movie tickets at $8.00 and rising, this is an important discount if you enjoy going to the movies.

Fairs and Expos

Festivals, expos, state and country fairs, circuses, and special interest shows also offer substantial discounts for seniors. Auto shows, house and garden shows, antique shows, holiday fairs, ski shows, recreational vehicle shows, boat shows, travel shows, arts and crafts shows, gift shows, and even air shows often have senior discounts on admission prices.

Eat for Cheap (or Free)

Over the past several years, the restaurant industry has found it pays to be good to their older patrons, who are among the largest percentage of repeat customers.

A simple way to eat for cheap, in fact for free, is to patronize restaurants that have special "Happy Hours." These are held during the slow hours (usually between 4 and 6 P.M.) when restaurants are looking for business before the normal dinner rush. These establishments offer specially priced drinks and free hors d'oeurves that would easily make a tasty, filling meal. If you live in a large city, chances are that many of the different ethnic restaurants offer a "Happy Hour" to entice new customers to try their special type of cuisine. In fact, one restaurant in Venice, California advertises a "Sushi Happy Hour" during the week.

Restaurants with popular bars often feature a delicious array of free food that changes nightly. Although you have to order a drink, it needn't be an alcoholic one. Juices and soft drinks will do quite well. And the delicious rewards on the hors d'oeurves table are well worth the price of a drink. (By the way, if you are a football fan, don't forget "Monday Night Football." Look for bars and restaurants with large screen televisions that advertise "FREE" food for coming in to watch the game and have a drink.)

"Early Bird Dinners" and "Sunset Meals" are especially popular with budget-minded diners who value quality food at good prices. Generally, a main course, vegetable, dessert, and beverage are included at a price lower that what the main course alone would cost during regular hours. Although they apply to everyone, these meals are targeted to seniors who often prefer to eat their evening meal early (sometimes making it their main meal of the day). Most restaurants offer "Early Bird dinners" until 6:30 or 7:00 P.M.

Many individual restaurants offer senior citizen discounts on regular menu items or have a special senior menu with lower prices. Some feature two-for-one dinners (for seniors or anyone). You can usually find these specials in the restaurant section of your neighborhood newspaper or senior publication. If you are not sure whether a restaurant has a senior special, ask for it.

Several national and regional restaurant chains offer senior citizen discounts. A few, like Denny's, are especially interested in the preferences and concerns of their older patrons. And for good reason. Adults over 55 make up nearly one-third of all Denny's customers patronizing their 1,500 restaurants. Depending on the individual restaurant chain's policy, discounts may be identical everywhere or may differ slightly from location to location. The restaurant may issue "membership" cards valid at all locations to seniors who patronize them frequently. Here are some examples of senior discounts at national restaurant chains:

Applebee's www.applebees.com offers a 10 percent discount for adults 55 and over.

Arby's www.arbys.com offers a 10 to 20 percent food discount, a free beverage with your meal and free coffee. Age requirements may vary from 55 to 60+ depending on management's program. Not every location offers the discount program.

Baskin-Robbins 31 Flavors Ice Cream Stores offers 10 percent off for seniors.

Bob's Big Boy family restaurants offer 10 percent off any meal, at any time for anyone in a party that includes one person over 55. Bob's Big Boy Senior Discount Cards are valid at all locations.

Boston Market offers seniors a 10 percent discount.

Burger King. Selected restaurants offer 10 percent discounts, others offer free coffee and tea.

Carl's Jr. offers discounts for folks 55 and older.

Carrows has a special senior menu with discounted prices for those over 55.

Chili's Restaurants. Some locations offer discounts to seniors. The percentages and ages vary, so ask at your local restaurant.

Denny's has a Senior Menu, which includes smaller portions for breakfast, lunch and dinner items. There is also a nightly dinner special that changes every day.

Dunkin' Donuts offers discounts for seniors 55 and over.

Golden Corral www.goldencorral.net offers discounts to seniors 60 and over.

Hardee's www.hardees.com offers a 15 percent discount to seniors 55 and over. Available on Wednesdays.

HomeTown Buffet www.oldcountrybuffet.com offers seniors 60 and over a Senior Club Card, which allows them to pay a discounted price.

International House of Pancakes www.ihop.com offers 10 percent off items on the regular menu or you can order from a senior menu, which has smaller portions.

Jack in the Box offers discounts for folks 55 and older.

Kentucky Fried Chicken www.kfc.com offers a 10 percent discount and special prices on its buffet for seniors 55 and over.

Long John Silver's offers 10 percent off your order or a discounted beverage price for seniors over 55.

Many McDonald's offer senior discounts. Ages and locations vary, so check with your local McDonald's.

Mrs. Fields Cookies offers a 10 percent discount to seniors over 60, but you have to ask for it.

Pizza Hut offers senior discounts at some locations. You can also print out discount coupons at their web site: www.pizzahut.com.

Residence Inn by Marriott. Adults 62 or older receive 15 percent off room rates according to availability. Breakfast is complimentary with room stay.

Shoney's offers a 10 percent discount for seniors 60 and over. Available every day.

Sizzler restaurants. Many locations offer discounts to seniors. They also offer savings to AARP members.

Taco Bell www.tacobell.com offers free drinks every day for seniors.

TCBY www.tcby.com frozen yogurt stores offer seniors the "Golden Discount Program" giving them 10 percent off the price of a single menu item and 20 percent off items through promotional mailing programs.

Wendy's offers 10 percent off or a discounted drink price for folks 55 or older.

Here are some examples of senior discounts at regional chain stores:

Coco's Bakery Restaurant www.cocosbakery.com has a Club 55 menu with discounted prices for seniors 55+. Locations in Arizona, California, Colorado, Nevada, and Washington.

Elephant Bar Restaurant www.elephantbar.com offers seniors 60 and over a 20 percent discount. Locations in California and the Midwest.

Fresh Choice www.freshchoice.com cafeterias offer a 10 percent senior discount. Locations in Texas, California, and Washington.

Friendly's has a discounted senior menu for diners over 60 that comes with a free side: either a cup of fresh coffee with breakfast or a Happy Ending Sundae for lunch or dinner. On the East Coast.

Le Peep Restaurants offers seniors a 10 percent discount with their Golden Years Club card. For locations, visit their web site: www.lepeep.com.

Picadilly has a Prime Time for Seniors Card and all adults over 60 get 10 percent off Monday through Saturday from 2–5 P.M. In the South.

Ponderosa Steakhouses www.ponderosasteakhouses.com offer a discounted senior menu for people 55 and over. Locations on the East Coast and in the Midwest.

Silver Diner restaurants offer seniors a 10 percent discount. Early bird specials from 4–6 P.M. are also available. Locations in Maryland, Virginia, and New Jersey.

Souper Salad www.soupersalad.com. Customers 60 and over receive a 10% discount with the Souper Salad Senior Card. Locations in the southwest and southeast.

Strings Italian Café www.stringscafe.com offers a 10% to 15% discount to seniors 55 and over. Ages and locations vary. Restaurants in California and Nevada.

Savings at Unusual Restaurants

Some combination dinner/theater attractions also give seniors a break. These include:

Arabian Nights Dinner Attraction www.arabian-nights.com in Kissimmee, Florida offers discounts to AARP members, or a $10 off coupon on their web site. E-mail: sales@arabian-nights.com. Or call 800-553-6116 (toll free USA), 800-553-3615 (toll free Canada), 407-239-9223 (Orlando/Kissimmee).

Hornblower Dining Yachts. 888-HORNBLOWER, www.hornblower.com. Operates in California harbors. 10 percent senior citizen discounts on dining cruises in Los Angeles and San Francisco, $2 off in San Diego.

Lake Tahoe Cruises www.zephyrcove.com. Lake Tahoe, California. 775-589-4906. Seniors (60 and over) receive a $3 per person discount on any *M.S. Dixie II* or *Tahoe Queen* cruise. Choose from a wide selection of breakfast, lunch, and dinner cruises. Ask for your discount when purchasing tickets. Address: 750 Highway 50, Zephyr Cove, NV 89448. Or make online reservations at: www.zephyrcove.com/reservations/cruise.cfm.

Medieval Times. 888-WE-JOUST, www.medieval times.com. Seven locations around the country. 10 percent off for senior citizens, and an additional 10 percent if you are an AAA member.

Tourist Attractions

Most tourist attractions around the country give special rates to senior visitors. Members of local or regional senior citizen organizations and clubs may also be entitled to special savings off entrance fees. Many attractions advertise special "limited time only" discounts for seniors at certain times of the year. These special promotions are often lower than the regular senior discounts. Some well-known U.S. attractions that offer senior citizen discounts include:

Audobon Zoo www.audoboninstitute.org. New Orleans, Louisiana. 504-581-4629 or 800-774-7394.

The senior discount is $2 off the regular admission price. The Audobon Nature Institute also offers discounts on its other attractions: the Aquarium of the Americas and the Entergy IMAX Theatre.

Boot Hill Museum www.boothill.org. Dodge City, Kansas. 316-227-8188. The senior discount is fifty cents off the regular adult ticket price. Off-season senior admission is $6.50. From Memorial Day through Labor Day senior admission is $7.50. Your admission ticket gives you access to view all of the exhibits and buildings in the Boot Hill Museum complex. Additional tickets must be purchased in the Boot Hill Museum gift shop and the General Rath Store. Further information email: frontst@pld.com.

Coral Reef State Park. Key Largo, Florida. 305-451-1202.

The Empire State Building www.esbnyc.com. New York, New York. 212-736-3100. Senior discount price is $14.76.

Gatorland. Orlando, Florida. 407-855-5496 or 1-800-393-JAWS. They offer 20 percent discount for seniors.

Grand Canyon Caverns, between Kingman and Seligman, Arizona. 502-422-3223/3224. Offers AARP discounts.

Meteor Crater. Flagstaff, Arizona. 800-842-7293. Offers $2 off for folks 60+.

New Orleans Steamboat Company www.steam boatnatchez.com. New Orleans, Louisiana. 800-233-BOAT.

Palm Springs Aerial Tramway www.pstramway.com. Palm Springs, California. 888-515-TRAM. Senior discount price is $19.95, 60 years and over.

Queen Mary www.queenmary.com. 1126 Queens Highway, Long Beach, California. 562-435-3511. Offers discounted AARP cabin rates.

Santa's Workshop, North Pole www.santas-colo.com. Colorado Springs, CO. 719-684-9432. Free admission to seniors 60+.

Spruce Goose. Located at the Evergreen Aviation Museum in McMinnville, OR offers discounts to those over 65. 3685 NE Three Mile Lane, McMinnville, OR. 503-434-4180.

The United Nations www.un.org/tours. New York, New York. 212-963-4475. Senior discount price is $9.00.

All three major television networks invite viewers to see their favorite shows:

ABC Tickets www.abc.abcnews.go.com/site/tvtickets.html. 4151 Prospect Avenue, Hollywood, CA 90027. See web site for where to write for specific shows.

CBS Tickets: 7800 Beverly Blvd., Los Angeles, CA 90036. See web site for where to write for specific shows.

NBC Tickets www.nbc.com/nbc/footer/Tickets. 3000 W. Alameda Blvd., Burbank, CA 91523.

Many tickets are also available through TV Tickets www.tvtickets.com, also known as Audiences Unlimited. They have a calendar of television program taping schedules. Order tickets by phone if you do not have Internet access: 818-753-3470 ext. 812.

Visit a Magic Kingdom for Less

People of all ages are fascinated by amusement and theme parks. For most of us, one visit is never enough. I love going with my children, my grandchildren, my friends and, of course, out of town guests. Most amusement parks offer senior citizen discounts. Disney offers the Disney Club, which gives discounts to anyone who purchases it. It is good for discounts on parking, meals, shops, some Hilton Hotels and National Car Rental locations. Members also receive a quarterly newsletter and vacation packages at Walt Disney World, Disneyland and other locations.

A sampling of other major amusement/theme parks that offer senior discounts include:

Adventure Island www.adventureisland.com. Tampa, Florida. 813-988-5171.

Busch Gardens www.buschgardens.com. Tampa, Florida. 813-987-5082. Senior discounts are available to anyone 55 and older.

Cedar Point www.cedarpoint.com. Sandusky, Ohio. 419-626-0830.

Cypress Gardens. Tampa, Florida. 800-282-2123. Senior discount price is $39.95.

Dorney Park www.dorneypark.com. Allentown, Pennsylvania. 610-395-3724. Senior discounts for those 62 or over.

Hershey Park www.hersheypark.com. Hershey, Pennsylvania. 800-HERSHEY. Hotel Hershey 800-533-3131. Senior discount price is $26.95 for anyone age 55–69, or $18.95 for age 70 and over. Gardens $9.00 for those 62 and over. Overnight stays are discounted with AARP memberships. Email: info@hersheypa.com for more information.

Holiday World www.holidayworld.com. Santa Claus, Indiana. 877-GO-FAMILY. Senior discount price is $29.95.

Knott's Berry Farm www.knotts.com. Buena Park, California. 714-220-5200. Senior prices for those over 61, including local resident special prices.

Legoland California. Carlsbad, California. 760-918-5346.

Sea World. 800-334-5722 or 407-351-3600 (Orlando, Florida). All Sea Worlds offer Senior discounts. For information on marine animals, visit their award-winning educational Web site at www.seaworld.org.

Silver Springs, Florida www.silversprings.com. 352-236-2121.

Universal Studios www.universalorlando.com. Orlando, Florida. 407-363-8000. Hollywood, California. 818-777-3762. Or toll free: 800-UNIVERSAL.

Wet 'n Wild www.wetnwildorlando.com. Orlando, Florida. 407-351-WILD or 800-992-WILD. Greensboro, North Carolina. 336-852-9721 or 800-555-5900. Senior discount price is $32.95 for anyone 60 and over.

Watch and Wager for Less
The races (dog and horse) are another exciting pastime that is popular among mature adults. Race courses around the country offer senior discounts, free "senior" days, "senior matinees" and "half-price" senior discounts. A few tracks offering discounts include the following (check your local race courses for discounts):

Churchill Downs www.churchilldowns.com. Louisville, Kentucky. 800-28-DERBY. 502-636-4400.

Daytona Beach Kennel Club www.daytonagrey
hound.com. Daytona Beach, Florida. 386-252-6484.
Seniors are admitted free on live racing matinees.

Earl Warren Showgrounds www.earlwarren.com.
Santa Barbara, California. 805-687-0766.

Golden Gate Fields www.goldengatefields.com.
Berkeley, California. 510-559-7300. Seniors 62 and over
with a Thoroughbreds card will receive a discount on
regular admission. Cards are available at the Customer Service booth. Free Grandstand or Club House
Admission every Thursday for seniors.

Hollywood Park www.hollywoodpark.com. Seniors
62 and over pay $4 general admission on Wednesdays
and Thursdays only. 310-419-1500.

If You're Looking for Culture

From art, science and industry, natural history,
and sports museums to zoos, botanical gardens, plan-
etariums, and historical landmarks, seniors will find
a wide array of educational and cultural attractions
that offer senior discounts throughout the year. They
are found in every city in the country, rural areas, and
out-of-the-way places. Astounding, awesome, and
breathtaking, the treasures, beauty and experiences
of these places will fill your days with wonderful and
lasting memories.

Besides the fact that many government-run institutions and establishments admit seniors for free

(including rides, special exhibits, transportation and events inside the attractions) these places offer interesting and stimulating insights into how this country was founded and built. Check with individual organizations for pertinent information including days and hours, senior discounts, "free" days, wheelchair access, current exhibits and special programs, membership information and services, guided tours, etc. Remember, always ask for your discount and present your identification before paying admission.

If you're visiting New York, you should definitely think about purchasing a CityPass www.citypass.net. With CityPass, you can visit six famous New York City museums and attractions for one low price. In addition to the American Museum of Natural History, the following attractions are included in the CityPass: Empire State Building Observatory, The Guggenheim Museum, Intrepid Sea Air Space Museum, and the Museum of Modern Art. CityPass can be purchased at any museum entrance and is good for 9 days from the date of purchase.

Cultural Attractions

Arlington National Cemetery www.arlingtoncem etery.org. Arlington, Virginia. 703-607-8000. Free admission. Nominal charge for parking.

Berkeley Municipal Rose Gardens. Berkeley, California. 510-644-6530.

Betsy Ross House www.ushistory.org/betsy/flag home.html. Philadelphia, Pennsylvania. 215-686-1252. Suggested donation, $5 adults, $2 children.

Birch Aquarium www.aquarium.ucsd.edu. La Jolla, California. 858-534-FISH. Senior discount for folks 60 and over.

Birmingham Museum of Art www.artsbma.org. Birmingham, Alabama. 205-254-2566.

California Academy of Sciences www.calacademy. org. San Francisco, California. 415-321-8000.

California African American Museum www.caam. ca.gov. Los Angeles, California. 213-744-7432.

California Science Center www.casciencectr.org. Los Angeles, California. 213-744-7400. Admission is free, $6 charge for parking.

California State Capitol Building (tour). 10th and L Streets. Sacramento, California. 916-324-0333.

Chicago Mercantile Exchange www.cme.com. Chicago, Illinois. E-mail for information: cme-tours@ cme.com.

Davy Crockett Birthplace State Park. Limestone, TN. 423-257-2167.

Death Valley National Monument. Death Valley, California. 760-786-3200. Seniors 62+ can use a Senior Pass for free entry.

The Franklin Institute Science Museum www2. fi.edu. Philadelphia, Pennsylvania. 215-448-1200. Discounts for seniors 62 and over.

Haleakala National Park, Haleakala, Hawaii. 808-572-4400. Seniors 62+ can use a Senior Pass for free entry.

Hawaii Volcanoes National Park. Hawaii. 808-985-6000. Senior Passes admitted for a free entry.

Huntington Library www.huntington.org. San Marino, California. 626-405-2100.

Independence Hall www.nps.gov/inde/index.htm. Philadelphia, Pennsylvania. 215-965-2305.

J. Paul Getty Museum www.getty.edu. Los Angeles, California. 310-440-7300. Admission is free. Parking is $8 per car.

Johnson Space Center www.nasa.gov/centers/johnson/home/index.html. Houston, Texas. 281-244-2100 for visitor information.

Lincoln Home National Historic Site www.nps.gov/liho. Springfield, Illinois. 217-492-4241, ext. 266 for the Visitor Center.

Montezuma National Wildlife Refuge www.fws. gov/r5mnwr. Seneca Falls, New York. 315-568-5987.

Mount Rushmore National Memorial www.nps.gov/ moru. Keystone, South Dakota. 605-574-2523. There is a one-time parking fee, for which Golden Age Passports are not accepted.

NASA Visitors Center www.nasa.gov/about/visiting/ index.html.

National Hall of Fame for Famous American Indians www.artcom.com/museums/nv/mr/73055.htm. Anadarko, Oklahoma. 405-247-5555.

National Museum of Naval Aviation www.navalavia tionmuseum.org. Pensacola, Florida. 850-452-3604.

Redwood National Park www.nps.gov/redw. Crescent City, California. 707-464-6101.

Temple Square www.lds.org/placestovisit. Salt Lake Temple, the Tabernacle. Salt Lake City, Utah. Toll free: 800-537-9703 or call 801-240-4872.

The Alamo www.thealamo.org. San Antonio, Texas. 210-225-1391.

Tomb of the Unknown Soldier. Arlington, Virginia. 703-607-8000.

Ulysses S. Grant Home www.granthome.com. Galena, Illinois. 815-777-3310. E-mail for information: granthome@granthome.com.

University of California Botanical Garden http://botanicalgarden.berkeley.edu. Also on the UC Berkeley grounds are an art museum, the Worth Ryder Gallery, an herbarium, and a paleontology museum. Berkeley, California. 510-643-2755. Senior discount price: $5 (65 and over). Free the first Thursday of every month.

U.S. Coast Guard Academy www.cga.edu. New London, Connecticut. Toll free: 800-883-USCG (8724) or call 860-444-8500.

Valley Forge National Historical Park www.nps.gov/VAFO. King of Prussia, Pennsylvania. 610-783-1077.

West Point Museum www.usma.edu/museum. West Point, New York. 914-938-4041. E-mail information: museum@usma.edu.

Wright Brothers National Memorial www.nps.gov/wrbr. Kill Devil Hills, North Carolina. 252-473-2111.

Washington, D.C. for Free

Our nation's capital, Washington, D.C., has more than three dozen free places of interest, museums, and historical sites, including The Bureau of Engraving and Printing, The F.B.I., Ford's Theater and Lincoln

Museum, The Kennedy Center, The Library of Congress, The National Gallery of Art, The Smithsonian Institution Group Museums, The Capitol, The White House, The National Archives, etc. This city is like a giant candy store full of free and exciting sights. For a free booklet that describes major attractions, information on parking, neighborhoods, The Metro, theaters, etc. write: D.C. Convention and Visitors Association, Attn: Tourist Info, 901 7th Street NW, 4th Floor, Washington, DC 20001. Or phone 800-422-8644 to request a free guide to the area, or fill out a form online (see "Contact Us") at their web site: www. washington.org.

Tours of the White House are now regulated. Call 202-456-7041 for the latest information on who can tour and when tours are offered. Group reservations must be made through your state Senator or Representative. To contact your representative, write Office of Senator (Name), United States Senate, Washington, DC 20510, or Office of Representative (Name), United States House of Representatives, Washington, DC 20515. You can also visit the official White House web site at: www.whitehouse.gov.

Nature

Dallas Zoo www.dallas-zoo.org. Dallas, Texas. 214-670-5656. Seniors $5, Regular Admission $8.75.

Indianapolis Zoo www.indyzoo.com. Indianapolis, Indiana. 317-630-2001. Discounts are offered. The zoo operating hours and admission prices vary by season.

Milwaukee County Zoo www.milwaukeezoo.org. Milwaukee, Wisconsin. 414-771-5500. Admission prices vary by season, but seniors always receive a discount of at least $1.00 off per ticket.

Monterey Bay Aquarium www.mbayaq.org. Monterey, California. 831-648-4800. Seniors $22.95 (65 and over). Disabled $15.95. Regular admission $24.95.

The National Aquarium www.aqua.org. Baltimore, Maryland. 410-576-3800. Seniors age 60 and older $20.95. Regular admission $21.95.

The Oakland Zoo www.oaklandzoo.org. Oakland, California. 510-632-9525. Seniors 55 and over $6. Regular admission $9.50.

Philadelphia Zoo www.philadelphiazoo.org. Philadelphia, Pennsylvania. 215-243-1100. You can get a discount with the Philadelphia CityPass.

Shaw Nature Reserve www.shawnature.org. Gray Summitt, Missouri. 636-451-3512. Seniors 65 and older $2. $3 regular admission.

John G. Shedd Aquarium www.sheddaquarium.org. Chicago, Illinois. 312-939-2438. Senior discount price $17.95 (65 and over). Regular admission $24.95.

The Steinhart Aquarium www.calacademy.org/aquarium. San Francisco, California. 415-750-7145. Senior discount price $6.50. Regular admission $10.00.

Museums

American Museum of Natural History and Rose Center for Earth and Space www.amnh.org. New York, New York. 212-769-5100. Senior discount price $11. Regular admission $15.

Art Institute of Chicago www.artic.edu. Chicago, Illinois. 312-889-5100. Seniors 65 and over $7. Regular admission $12.

Autry National Center www.autry-museum.org. Los Angeles, California. 323-667-2000. Senior discount price $5. Regular admission $9. The second Tuesday of every month is free.

Aviation Museum www.amszp.org, Santa Paula Airport, East Santa Maria Street, Santa Paula, CA. 805-525-1109. Admission is free.

The B & O Railroad Museum www.borail.org. Baltimore, Maryland. 410-752-2490. $12 for seniors 60 and over. $14 for adults.

Denver Art Museum www.denverartmuseum.org. Denver, Colorado. 720-865-5000. Senior discount price $10. Regular admission $13.

Fine Arts Museums of San Francisco www.thinker.org. San Francisco, California. The de Young, Legion of Honor. 415-750-3600. Senior discount price $7. Regular admission $10. Free admission the first Tuesday of each month.

Frank Lloyd Wright Home and Studio www.wright plus.org. Oak Park, Illinois. 708-848-1978. Senior discount price $10 (65 and over). Regular admission $12.

International Museum of Photography and Film at the George Eastman House www.eastmanhouse.org. Rochester, New York. 585-271-3361. Senior discount price for 60 and older $6. Regular admission $8.

The Jewish Museum www.jewishmuseum.org. New York, New York. 212-423-3200. Senior discount price $10. Regular admission $12. Free admission on Saturdays.

Los Angeles County Museum of Art www.lacma.org. Los Angeles, California. 323-857-6000. Senior discount price $5 (62 and over). Regular admission $9.

The Metropolitan Museum of Art www.metmuse um.org. New York, New York. 212-535-7710. Suggested senior citizen admission $15. Adult admission $20.

Monticello www.monticello.org. Charlottesville, Virginia. 434-984-9822. Admission $15. No senior discount.

Museum of Arts & Design www.madmuseum.org. New York, New York. 212-956-3535. Senior discount price $7. Regular admission $9.

Museum of Contemporary Art San Diego www. mcasd.org. La Jolla, California. 858-454-3541. Senior discount price $5. Regular admission $10. Free admission the third Tuesday of each month.

Museum of Modern Art www.moma.org. New York, New York. 212-708-9400. Senior discount price $16 (65 and over). Regular admission $20. Friday from 4:00–8:00 P.M., admission is free.

National Air and Space Museum www.nasm.si.edu. Washington DC. 202-633-1000. Admission is free.

National Cowboy & Western Heritage Museum www.nationalcowboymuseum.org. Oklahoma City, Oklahoma. 405-478-2250. Senior discount price $7. Regular admission $8.50.

Page Museum www.tarpits.org, Los Angeles, California. 323-934-PAGE (7243). Senior discount price $4.50 (62 and over). Regular admission $7. Free admission the first Tuesday of each month.

The Paul Revere House www.paulreverehouse.org. Boston, Massachusetts. 617-523-2338. Senior discount price $2.50. Regular admission $3.

The Solomon R. Guggenheim Museum www.guggenheim.org. New York, New York. 212-423-3500. Senior discount price $15. Regular admission $18.

University Museum of Archaeology and Anthropology www.museum.upenn.edu. Philadelphia, Pennsylvania. 215-898-4000. Senior donation $5. Regular donation $8.

Whitney Museum of American Art www.whitney. org. New York, New York. 800-WHITNEY. Senior discount price $10. Regular admission $15.

The performing arts are also popular activities where seniors get a break. From theater, symphony, and ballet, to circuses and acrobatic troupes, seniors can enjoy many days and nights of first-class, first-run professional performances at special discounted rates from 25 to 50 percent off regular priced tickets. In the past several years, ticket prices have risen markedly, reaching $70 to $125 for single tickets. Most senior discounts offer significant savings that are sometimes greater at matinees and less popular performances.

There are also "rush" tickets that go on sale the day of a performance that are often 50 percent or more off the face price. A popular theater at the Music Center in Los Angeles offers $10 Public Rush Tickets that are available 10 minutes before curtain time. That's a 75 percent savings off the lowest price $40 ticket! Also, check for preview performance discounts prior to official public openings. This same theater in Los Angeles was offering the best seats in the house for $20 during the preview period. If you can get several people together, you may qualify for senior group rates with reduced prices. Some performing art organizations even offer special "senior performances" and "senior afternoon concerts." Again, it's important to inquire with box office personnel about all the possible savings opportunities before you purchase your tickets.

Sporting Events

Football, baseball, basketball, tennis, track and field, hockey, etc., generally take place in stadiums, auditoriums, and arenas that offer senior discounts for sport events held there during the year. The same stadium may be home to more than one team or host several independent events throughout the year. Check with the office of the teams or the public relations department at the stadium for individual and group senior discounts, year-round discount cards, or special membership opportunities. During regular playing season, there are often one or more senior citizen days. Many teams will even give freebies (pennants, caps, souvenirs) to seniors who ask for them. These are advertised in the local newspaper and in the team's season calendar listing special events and dates. Individual and special multi-day sports events also offer senior citizen discounts.

Also, if you're a real fan, write to your favorite team for a free fan package that generally includes team photos, calendars of games, decals and more. Send a postcard or self-addressed stamped envelope and they will mail you back a goodie package for free. You can look up your team in your phone book, write or call the league headquarters, or call the arena or stadium where they play their home games.

CHAPTER 2

Sports, Fitness and Exercise

As we move deeper into the twenty-first century, it is obvious that our society will continue to place a great deal of emphasis on fitness and exercise. This is especially true for seniors, as local, state, and national programs continue to thrive with the increase in participation by this age group. Pick up any magazine or newspaper targeted for seniors and you will find numerous opportunities to engage in healthful exercise programs and sports activities. Exercise is not only accepted, but it is strongly encouraged by every major medical association and organization for healthy seniors who want to live longer, fuller lives. In fact, it is nearly impossible to find a sport today that is not being enjoyed by older adults.

Along with the healthful benefits of participating in sports is the added benefit that most sports, exercise, and fitness programs can be enjoyed at substantially reduced prices. In fact, many charges are completely waived simply because you are a senior. Imagine spending a glorious day on the ski slopes for absolutely free, while others have spent up to $70 for a one-day lift ticket!

Calling All Athletes

The National Senior Games Association (formerly known as The U.S. National Senior Sports Organization) events have been held every two years since they began at Washington University in St. Louis in 1987. In order to compete, an athlete must be 55 years or older, and must qualify at a local or state competition sanctioned by the National Senior Games Association.

There are more than 500 separate events in archery, badminton, half-court basketball, bicycling, bowling, track and field, golf, horseshoes, race-walking, 5K and 10K road races, shuffleboard, softball, swimming, table tennis, tennis, volleyball, and the triathlon. Competitions are organized for men and women and are separated into age categories. For additional information on qualification requirements and schedules of qualifying games, contact: National Senior Games Association, P.O. Box 82059, Baton Rouge, Louisiana 70884-2059. 225-766-6800. Or look up their web site: www.nsga.com.

State Competitions

Several states hold their own senior games, some alternating seasons similar to the summer and winter Olympics. The games often take place at local college or state university campuses. Athletes competing in qualifying competitions at these games go on to participate in the National Senior Games. In addition to the states listed below, there are programs sponsored by county, city, and local agencies, which participate in the national program. Some state parks and recreation departments are also involved in senior competitions affiliated with the national games.

This web site has links to several states' senior games web sites, offices, and contacts: www.nsga.com/direct ory.html.

Arizona Senior Olympic Games. Held in Tucson (520-791-3244), Sierra Vista (520-458-7922), Yuma (928-373-5238), Green Valley (520-625-3440 x.216), Prescott (928-777-1122 x.0) and Flagstaff (928-774-1068). The 24th annual edition of the Arizona State Senior Olympic Games (ASO) were held in Phoenix in mid-Feb. 2006. For more information call the ASO office at 602-534-3500. www.seniorgames.org.

California Senior Olympics www.cvrpd.org/pro grams/seniorolympics.htm.

The Pasadena Senior Center offers Olympic programs: 85 E. Holly Street, Pasadena, CA 91103.

Colorado hosts the Rocky Mountain Senior Games twice a year, in summer and winter. Contact: Senior Sports Development Council, Greeley Senior Activity Center, 1010 6th Street, Greeley, CO 80631. 970-350-9433. Web site: www.greeleygov.com/RMSG/default.aspx.

Connecticut Senior Games. Contact: Connecticut Senior Games, Connecticut Sports Management Group, 290 Roberts Street, Suite 301, East Hartford, CT 06108.

Empire State Senior Games www.empirestategames. org/senior (formerly New York Senior Games) are held in the spring and are open to state residents up to 80+. Contact: New York State Office of Parks, Recreation and Historic Preservation—Central Region, 6105 E. Seneca Tpk., Jamesville, NY 13078-9516. 315-492-9654

Florida Senior Games www.flasports.com/page_sen iorgames.shtml are held in Cape Coral annually in December. Look on the web site for a list of locations for state championships or contact: Stephen Rodriguez, Florida Sports Foundation, 2930 Kerry Forest Parkway, Tallahassee, FL 32309. 866-FLGames or 850-488-8347.

Keystone State Games www.keystonegames.com (formerly Pennsylvania Senior Games) are a six-day event. Contact: Keystone State Games, P.O. Box 1166, Wilkes-Barre, PA 18703. 570-823-3164.

North Carolina holds local games throughout the state. Winners compete in the state finals in Raleigh. Contact: North Carolina Senior Games, P.O. Box 33590, Raleigh, NC 27636. 919-851-5456.

Oklahoma Senior Games www.oklahomasenior games.org. This is an exciting eight-day sports festival exclusively for men and women age 50 and over featuring 72 events in 22 different sports and two creative/literary art competitions. Oklahoma Senior Games, 1829 West Honolulu, Broken Arrow, OK 74012. E-mail: danamike98@valornet.com. 918-455-1894.

The Texas Senior Games Association can be reached at www.tsga.org. Or write: Kevin Beavers, 1909 Curtis B. Elliott Drive, Temple, TX 76501. 254-298-5407.

Vermont holds the Green Mountain Senior Games in early fall in Castleton, Vermont. Contact: Green Mountain Senior Games, 131 Holden Hill Road, Weston, VT 05161. 802-824-6521

Virginia Senior Games. Virginia Recreation and Park Society, 6038 Cold Harbor Road, Mechanicsville, VA 23111. 804-730-9447. E-mail: vsg@vrps.com.

For information on Washington Senior Games contact 360-413-0148 in Olympia.

Senior sports competitions are also held in Alabama, Arkansas, Georgia, Idaho, Illinois, Indiana, Iowa, Kansas, Kentucky, Louisiana, Maine, Maryland, Minnesota, Mississippi, Nebraska, Nevada, New Hampshire, New Jersey, New Mexico, Ohio, Rhode Island, South Carolina, South Dakota, Tennessee, Washington DC, Wisconsin, and Wyoming.

Since 1987 Huntsman Chemicals has sponsored the World Senior Games for senior athletes 50 and above each October in Utah. Senior athletes from all parts of the world are invited to participate in events including golf, swimming, bicycling, tennis, race-walking, track and field, softball, bowling, and racquetball. For information contact: Huntsman World Senior Games, 1070 West 1600 South, A-103, St. George, UT 84770. 800-562-1268. Web site: www.seniorgames.net.

The National Veterans Golden Age Games www1. va.gov/vetevent/gag/2007/Default.cfm. Veterans' groups across the country sponsor competition in a variety of events. Contact: National Veterans Golden Age Games, 50 Irving Street NW, Washington DC 20422. 713-794-8779.

Tennis—The Sport for a Lifetime

Senior tennis is a thriving and popular sport. There are senior tournaments and competitions held at every level of play. Check with your local parks and recreation department, health or tennis club for information on tournament play for seniors. Also, county tennis associations sponsor tournament play for seniors. If your local park or community center doesn't have an organized program, the United States Tennis Association has compiled a series of worksheets on its web site that shows how to launch teams of players of the same level of play. For more information you can contact the USTA at 70 West Red Oak Lane, White Plains, New York 10604. Or call: 914-696-7000.

The USTA holds Senior National Championships each year at tennis facilities throughout the country.

There are divisions for men's and women's singles and doubles, from age 30 through 85, Father-Son Doubles and Mother-Daughter Doubles. Write the USTA for their Senior National Championship brochure, which includes dates of play, locations, requirements, and fees. You can write for this guide and a complete list of current USTA Tennis publications at: USTA Publications Department, 70 West Red Oak Lane, White Plains, New York 10604. For additional information check out the USTA web site: www.usta.com.

The USTA Tennis League provides a framework for team competition at local levels, culminating in playoffs in which teams travel outside their local area playing a series of championships at district, sectional and national levels. The league offers senior competition in every USTA section of the United States except the Caribbean.

Run for Your Life

The Lifelong Fitness Alliance www.50plus.org promotes the exchange of information between the growing numbers of over-50 runners. Formed by researchers from Stanford University, the group also encourages studies of the effects and impact of running on different aspects of life. Members receive an excellent quarterly newsletter, *Fifty-Plus Bulletin*, and participate in continuing studies and surveys. Contact: Lifelong Fitness Alliance, 658 Bair Island Road, Suite 200, Redwood City, California 94063. Tel: 650-361-8282.

Road Runners Club of America www.rrca.org has over 450 local affiliates throughout the country. The popular "Run For Your Life" program, a physical fitness program, originated with this group. For brochures and information on their programs and services contact: RRCA, 1501 Lee Highway, Suite 140, Arlington, VA 22209. E-mail: execdir@rrca.org. Tel: 703-525-3890.

Another organization that promotes running is the American Running Association www.americanrunning.org. Write them for information at: 4405 East West Highway, Suite 405, Bethesda, Maryland 20814. Or call: 301-913-9517 or 800-776-2732.

Take Yourself Out to the Ball Game

Baseball is another popular senior sport enjoyed by over 200,000 people. The Senior Softball-USA promotes international interest in the game and sponsors teams throughout the country. Members receive a quarterly newsletter and have the opportunity of playing in a yearly national tournament and exhibition games and tournaments around the world. For information write: Senior Softball-USA, 2701 K Street, Suite 101A, Sacramento, California 95816.

If you do not wish to play, but love baseball, many of the major and minor league baseball teams offer senior discount days and reduced priced tickets for clubs. Check with the group ticket office of your local baseball team for these special offers.

The Amateur Softball Association www.softball.org provides information on local leagues and how to start up a softball league. They also coordinate tournaments for 50+ league players. Contact them at: 800-44-COACH.

If You're on a Roll, Bowl

Bowling is another great sport for seniors and has grown tremendously over the past decade. Senior leagues and tournaments are very popular, and most bowling alleys reduce game fees for both individuals and groups. Also, since bowling alleys are usually less crowded during the daytime hours, this is one of the best times for senior bowling. The American Bowling Congress www.bowl.com, ABC, Bowling Headquarters, 5301 South 76th Street, Greendale, WI 53129 will send you information on bowling for older adults and where there are leagues in your area. Toll free: 800-514-BOWL (2695).

If your local bowling alley is a member of the American Bowling Congress www.bowl.com or the Women's International Bowling Congress, you can ask them to send you the 12-part "Bowling for Seniors" packet, which contains ideas on starting leagues, scoring, tournaments, bowling film rentals, and other ideas on developing an active senior program. Or contact your neighborhood bowling center about joining their senior leagues.

Walk for Health

Probably the fastest growing active sport for older adults today is walking. The number of exercise walkers 55+ has more than doubled in recent years, from approximately 8.6 million in 1985 to more than 20 million. Not only is walking good for the heart, but it has also been established that it's good for the bones as well. A recent study found that through a regular schedule of walking, jogging, or climbing stairs, men and women can build stronger bones and help prevent osteoporosis, a disease prevalent in older adults, especially women. Women who exercise regularly can actually increase bone mass in the spine, helping give bones strength and resistance to fracture. The study also found that the typical serious walker is a 53-year old woman who walks an average of 15 miles a week.

Walking programs, clinics, and clubs can be found in almost every town and city in the country. Indoor shopping malls have become popular places to walk because of their safe environment and year-round availability, regardless of weather conditions. In addition, some organized clubs sponsor lectures on a wide range of health topics given by physicians and health professionals. From Walk-A-Dillies to Senior Strutters, there are community groups for walking in your area. Check with local senior citizen groups, "senior" newspapers, community centers and medical facilities to locate a walking club or program in your area.

WalkStyles is a national organization that promotes fitness through walking. Contact them at WalkStyles, Inc., 26062 Merit Circle, Suite 101, Laguna Hills, CA 92653.

You can also contact the Mall Walkers of America, P.O. Box 202434, Austing, TX 78720, or Walkways

Center, 733 15th Street, NW, Suite 427, Washington, DC 20005 for information on their organizations.

If you live in San Francisco contact: The Walk-a-block Club of San Francisco. 925-373-4816. Web site: www.walkablock.com.

In Southern California, check out Southern California Walkers, 626-795-3243 or e-mail at narwf@sbcglobal.net to receive coaching in the proper race walking techniques. The Walkers Club of LA, 818-763-3208 (or e-mail nanalex@earthlink.net) meets each Sunday morning. Another organization that provides walking opportunities for seniors in the area is the Sierra Club http://angeles.sierraclub.org or 213-387-4287. For scenically oriented walkers, Coastwalk at 800-550-6854 or www.coastwalk.org offers a series of weeklong regional hikes each summer and year-round daily hikes along the Pacific coastline. If you want to start your own walking club, contact Tom Pontac of Leisure Leggers at 562-430-5777.

Start a Mall-Walkers Program for Senior Citizens. Go to: www.ndep.nih.gov/diabetes/pubs/ComPart Guide_Senior.pdf. This online tip sheet tells you how to start your own mall-walking program.

If you live in New York, check out The New York Walkers Club. In Manhattan the group meets every Saturday, at 9:30 A.M. in Central Park near the 90th Street and 5th Avenue entrance. Look for their banner. Clinics/workouts last for about 75 minutes. For beginner, intermediate, and advanced healthwalkers, and racewalkers. 516-579-WALK. www.nywalkersclub.org.

In Queens the group meets Saturdays at 9:00 A.M. at the Victory Field track, Myrtle Avenue and Woodhaven Boulevard. Warm-ups and cool-downs are at the track and workouts are on the track and on the adjacent Forest Park roadway. For beginners and intermediates.

In Long Island the Long Island Walkers Club meets every Saturday at 8:00 A.M. at Eisenhower Park, East Meadow in front of the Fieldhouse adjacent to the tennis courts at Parking Field 2. Use Hempstead Turnpike Entrance. Clinics/ workouts last about 75 min. For beginner, intermediate, and advanced health-walkers and racewalkers. www.longislandwalkers.free servers.com.

In Vermont check out Country Walkers www.coun trywalkers.com. P.O. Box 180, Waterbury, Vermont. 800-464-9255 / 802-244-1387. For a brochure on their walking tours around the world e-mail at info@coun trywalkers.com.

The Rockport Walking Institute offers a free walking brochure, "The Rockport Guide to Fitness Walking." The brochure contains a self-administered fitness assessment and a 20-week walking program designed for various fitness levels and ages. Write them at: 220 Donald Lynch Blvd., P.O. Box 480, Marlboro, MA 01752. Or call 800-762-5767 and ask for the Rockport Fitness Walking Institute.

For information on race-walking and other walking events, contact the USA Track & Field (USATF) (formerly The Athletics Congress) www.usatf.org. For information on "Elite Athletes" from ages 30 to 100+ and their programs, contact: Sariyn "Beka" Suggs, Director of Elite Athletic Programs. E-mail: Sariyu. Suggs@ usatf.org. 317-261-0500.

Finally, there are several good books and pamphlets available on walking including:

Walking Magazine: The Complete Guide to Walking for Health, Fitness, and Weight Loss, by Mark Fenton, published by Globe Pequot Press.

Fitness Walking, by Therese Iknoian, Human Kinetics Publishing.

Fitness Walking for Dummies, by Liz Neporent, For Dummies Press.

The Classic Game of Golf

Although seniors have been aware of it for decades, the game of golf has enjoyed an international resurgence, in part due to the tremendous popularity it found among the Japanese during the '80s and '90s. In the United States, the game has grown in popularity because of charismatic golf champions like Tiger Woods. Most public and many private golf courses will give a discount on greens fees for seniors over 65.

The Golf Card www.golfcard.com which costs $65 a year for single membership and $99 for a couple, was designed especially with seniors in mind. It entitles members to play two free rounds of 18-hole golf at nearly 3,400 member golf courses around the world. As a Golf Card bearer, you also receive Golf Traveler magazine, a directory and guide to member courses and resorts participating in the program, as well as discounts on golf vacation packages at nearly 400 member resorts. There is no minimum age requirement to join the program, however the average age of members is 61. Contact: Golf Card International, 64 Inverness Drive E, Englewood, CO 80112. 800-321-8269.

The Senior Golfers Association of America (SGA) www.seniorgolfersamerica.com participates in golfing tournaments across the country. The SGA also sends out a quarterly newsletter with detailed information about the tournaments, which include the Senior Amateur Championships of America, Palm Springs Classic, Pacific Northwest Championship, Tournament of Oranges, and the Blue Ridge Classic. For more information write: SGA, 3013 Church Street, Myrtle Beach, SC 29577. 843-626-8100.

The National Senior Golf Association www.nsg tour.com. 3673 Nottingham Way, Hamilton Square, NJ 08690. 800-282-6772. This organization has organized and conducted vacation golf tournaments at some of the world's premier resorts for more than 20 years. You must be at least 50 years old to qualify for tournament awards. There are several benefits offered with membership including discounts on golf equipment, auto rental discounts, a newsletter, a Hale Irwin Golf

Passport and more. Annual membership is $35 with a three-year membership at $75.

Many senior golf competitions and tournaments are held by public and private organizations and clubs throughout the year. Charities have found that sponsoring senior golf tournaments is a great way to raise funds and enlist older adults in a healthy, fun activity. Many regular tournaments advertise special senior discounts for daily or multi-day passes. For instance, daily ground passes for the weeklong Nissan Los Angeles Open (formerly the Los Angeles Open Golf Tournament) cost $25 per day. Senior passes are $20 per day, adding up to some good savings if you plan to attend several days. Check with public golf courses, Departments of Parks and Recreation, and senior publications for their local activities, tournaments, and senior discounts.

You're Never Too Old to Ski

Skiing is a very popular sport among older adults, and there are several clubs and discounts specifically targeted for this age group. For those taking up the sport for the first time, or for veteran skiers who have been schussing down the slopes for decades, with great deals available for seniors, this may be the best time of all to enjoy this exciting sport. Here are some clubs and organization you should contact:

The Over The Hill Gang http://othgi.com. This group (its motto: "Once you're over the hill, you pick up speed") originated with a group of older skiers looking for other older skiers to ski with. They are now an international skiing group with over 6,500 members in all 50 states and 13 countries. They accept members starting at age 50, and promise major discounts. Members not affiliated with local groups can obtain lifetime memberships for $345 (for members 63 and over) and $515 (for members 50 to 62); most group members pay $125 for three years, $50 for one year, and join periodic ski tours with the group (they also go on sporting-type summer trips). They also offer a yearly Senior Ski Week that takes place at a ski resort in the Rockies or Europe and week-long vacation packages at several resorts around Lake Tahoe, California. Local Gang groups also organize ski trips with their own members or meet to ski weekly at local ski resorts. For information on membership write: Over the Hill Gang International, 1515 North Tejon Street, Colorado Springs, CO 80907, or call 719-389-0022.

70+ Ski Club. If you can prove you are over 70, you can join the 70+Ski Club, founded by the remarkable Lloyd Lambert, who skied up until his death at the age of 96. The group now boasts over 17,000 members. One of the original purposes of this group was to make skiing more affordable for older adults on fixed or limited retirement incomes. Club members meet as a group every year for an annual meeting and participate in the 70+ Ski Races at Hunter Mountain in the Catskills. Cost of an annual membership is $10, and includes a newsletter and list of ski areas across the country offering free or discounted skiing for seniors. For information write directly to Lloyd's son Richard, who personally registers new members: 1633 Albany Street, Schenectady, NY 12304. 518-346-5505. E-mail: rtl70plus@aol.com

If you ski in the east, there are several ski clubs organized for older adults:

• Stratton Trailblazers www.strattontrailblazers. com (formerly Stratton Senior Skiers Association). Contact the group by e-mail to learn more about their activities: info@strattontrailblazers.com.

• Waterville Valley Silver Streaks www.waterville. com/info/winter/silverstreaks.asp.

• Get Off Your Rockers is an activities club for seniors based in San Diego that provides several ski trips each year to Mammoth and out of state. Contact: GOYR, 16320 Roca Drive, San Diego, CA 92128 or call 858-472-3231.

Sundance Senior Ski Group. For information on their activities in Utah, call Glenn McGettigan at 801-375-1322.

Ski resorts throughout the country offer older adults discounts on tickets, rentals, and other amenities. Many discounts range from 50 percent off lift tickets to free tickets and season passes for adults over 55. For example, 46 ski areas or resorts in Michigan offer free downhill or cross-country skiing to people over 55. If you are thinking of taking a ski vacation, check the discounts on vacation packages at hotels and ski lodges associated with the ski area's operators. Always ask about the senior discounts before purchasing daily lift tickets or tickets included with tours and vacation packages.

Even if you don't ski, how about taking the grand-children on a ski vacation, sharing in the fun and action, and perhaps taking a lesson as well? Weekdays are often slow times at ski resorts, and many offer midweek family plans at greatly reduced rates, often including free lodging (and sometimes lift passes) for the kids.

Cross-Country Skiing

Cross-country skiing is another popular form of exercise that provides an excellent aerobic workout, yet takes it easy on the joints. More than 6.5 million Americans enjoy this sport, which not only costs considerably less than downhill skiing, but also avoids annoying waits in long lift lines. Although many people believe that, "if you can walk, you can cross-country ski," it's not as simple as that. The Cross County Ski Areas Association recommends that everyone take a lesson or two to become familiar with the equipment and techniques. Check the web site for the CCSAA directory called "Resorts & Trails" that lists more than 200 cross-country ski areas, many of which offer discounts for seniors. For info write: Cross Country Ski Areas Association, 259 Bolton Road, Winchester, NH 03470. Web site: www.xcski.org.

For serious cross-country skiers, the World Masters Cross-country Ski Association www.world-masters-xc-skiing.ch sponsors yearly international races. Participants must be over 30, and events are separated into five-year age groups up to 80. For information contact: John Downing, Box 604, Bend, OR 97709. 541-317-0217. Or e-mail him at: jd@xcskiworld.com.

In addition to asking for senior discounts at the more than 800 cross-country ski areas around the country, there are a variety of special packages offered by travel companies. A few include:

The Aspen Skiing Company www.aspensnowmass.com offers senior discounts on lift tickets.

Outdoor Vacations for Women Over 40 offers cross-country ski clinics, weekend and longer packages for women who like adventurous outdoor vacations. Write: Women Over 40, P.O. Box 200, Groton, MA 01450. Or call: 508-448-3331.

Elderhostel www.elderhostel.org combines its educational programs with low-cost cross-country ski vacations near its educational sites. For information write: Elderhostel, 11 Avenue de Lafayette, Boston, MA 02111-1746. Or call: 877-426-8056.

Dancing
Dancing is by far the most popular social exercise enjoyed by older adults. It is fun, non-stressing,

friendly, and good for you. Look in the activities section of your local newspaper or "senior" newspaper and you will most likely find a senior dance event happening that same week. One Southern California senior citizen newspaper listed no fewer than 12 dance events. Weekly dances and dance classes are held at recreation centers, senior clubs, churches, and community centers.

Stay in Shape with Swimming

Swimming is often recommended for people with arthritis and back or leg injuries. Some fitness experts consider it the healthiest and best overall sport and all-around conditioner. In addition, swimming is one of the most injury-free sports because there is less stress on the joints and muscle system. It is also an inexpensive sport that does not require a lot of special equipment or training.

Swimming is so good for you, in fact, it has been the most popular participation sport in the United States for the past several years. For information on pool locations, lap times and classes contact your health club, YMCA, YWCA, local college, or city Parks and Recreation Department.

Volkssporting

The American Volkssport Association www.ava.org is a nonprofit, volunteer organization whose goal is to promote physical fitness and good health by encouraging all people, regardless of age, to exercise in noncompetitive, stress-free programs. Volkssports are organized, noncompetitive walking, swimming, bicycling and cross-country skiing events. Each event has a premarked scenic trail and/or measured distance designed to appeal to all ages. There are even special provisions for the handicapped to participate in most events. Participation is free of charge.

Volkssporting is an especially beneficial opportunity for seniors who cannot, should not, or simply don't want to exercise in timed or competitive events. Seniors have an equal chance to participate in programs of exercise and fun where no special training or equipment is required and at the same time is safe. Participants in the Lifesports program choose the sport(s), the distance(s), and the pace.

The American Volkssport Association has over 600 member clubs chartered in 50 states. The AVA publishes The American Wanderer, a bimonthly newsletter of Volkssporting news, calendar of events, AVA club list, and other information. For information write: American Volkssport Association, 1001 Pat Booker Road, Suite 101, Universal City, TX 78148.

Non-Stress Exercise

Not everyone is able to join in the sports and activities described in these last few pages. However, almost everyone can exercise in some way. Arthritis, one of the most common villains in the battle against growing older, limits millions from participating in the more vigorous, active sports. Range-of-motion exercises (for flexibility and range of movement), stretching, and strength-building programs are enthusiastically supported by the medical community for those having any of the more than 100 different rheumatic disorders. Here are some worthwhile organizations to look into:

The Arthritis Foundation www.arthritis.org has over 70 chapters throughout the country that offer free educational courses, exercise programs, and support resources. They also publish an exercise brochure filled with safety tips and examples of safe, range-of-motion exercises. For information contact: The Arthritis Foundation, P.O. Box 7669, Atlanta, Georgia 30357-0669. Toll free: 800-283-7800. 404-872-7100.

The American Physical Therapy Association www.apta.org features a free guide sheet with stretching tips to avoid some of the stiffness and minor pain associated with exercise and sports on their web site.

The National Institute on Aging www.nia.nih.gov has articles and other general information on how exercise can help you live a longer, healthier life. Look up their web site or contact: the National Institute on Aging Information Center, P.O. Box 8057, Gaithersburg, MD 20898-8057. 800-222-2225.

CHAPTER 3

"Time of Your Life" Travel

Welcome to the world of senior travel! Today's mature adults have more freedom to travel without the restrictions and responsibilities of children, busy households, complicated schedules, and building careers.

Traveling can be a learning experience, an adventure, a much deserved chance to relax, a physical challenge, or whatever you dream it to be. After waiting this many years, you can be flexible and travel wherever you want, as long as you want, and whenever you want. This translates into lots of savings because, in addition to year-round senior discounts, you can make your travel plans during those times when airline, hotel, car rental, cruise, etc., prices are at their lowest. By using the methods outlined in this chapter, you can save as much as 85 percent on fares and accommodations. Exotic island winter trips, distant European holidays, and cross-country visits to see the grandchildren are just a few of the possibilities. The "trip of a lifetime" can come more than once for mature adults who take advantage of the opportunities available to them.

Travel is the number one desire and activity of the 50+ age group. In fact, 80 percent of all pleasure travel is by individuals over 50. In addition, they take more trips per year, travel longer distances, and spend more time away from home than any other age group.

Every recent study has shown that the overwhelming bulk of all travel expenditures are made by people 50 years of age and over; the young have far less money and less time to travel. And within that 50-plus age group, the segment composed of persons 65 and older is growing faster than any other. Today's mature Americans remain vital and active for many more years than was formerly the case, and they want to travel.

As a result, seniors spend more money, on the whole, than anyone else. The travel industry has vigorously courted the mature adult market by creating numerous discount programs, tours, packages, etc., just for them. Travel agents, airlines, cruise lines, hotels, and other travel businesses know mature adults are free to travel at off-peak times or whenever they desire a change of scenery. They also know that this age group includes shrewd, experienced travelers who look for the best deals to the best places.

The travel industry has also reduced the burden of planning vacations by creating an array of choices and ways to travel, thus relieving seniors of the tedious details of "do it yourself" vacations. Even if you are an experienced traveler, planning a trip can become quite complicated. Yes, there are many excellent, money saving deals available, but rates, fares, and privileges can change at a moment's notice. There are such a variety of fares and accommodations, it's often difficult to know if you are really getting the most for your money. A travel agent can often save you more money than you'll spend when you plan a vacation yourself. Don't overlook these valuable professionals.

Traveling for Free

There are several ways mature adults can take advantage of the little-known "tricks of the trade" within the travel industry to earn free travel. Most free travel requires no special skills, credentials, or contacts. And it can be as luxurious and pleasurable as the most expensive paid vacation. Consider the following if you want to see the world and do it at somebody else's expense:

- Become a tour escort for a travel agency that operates tours; a senior citizen center or club with tour programs; or a professional tour operator. Tour operators are always looking for interesting people to lead their tours, especially during the summer tourist season. You will act as tour leader/manager for the group with all your expenses paid. If you are fluent in one or more languages, your services will be especially desirable for tours to foreign countries.

- Organize your own tour or group. If you can enlist enough people, you can get a whole trip, long or short, for free. Some travel agencies recruit teachers who receive a free trip if they bring six students. With 12 students, your spouse can join you for free. Traveling free as a teacher is a very popular way to visit places that would otherwise be financially prohibitive.

• Work for a travel agency. By becoming trained as a travel agent you can qualify for large travel discounts and free travel. Travel agents can often work part-time or from home and still receive the same benefits as full-time counselors.

• Organize a "special interest" tour. If you are a wine aficionado, you might organize a trip to the French wine country; or put together a group from your church for a religious pilgrimage to a Holy Land; or travel to Vienna and Salzburg with other opera buffs for the yearly music festival. Special-interest trips focus on everything from golf, tennis, and bicycling to photography, archaeology, history, theater, music, and gourmet food. A good travel agent can create a tour around your group's common interest. And by organizing and providing the travelers, you will earn a free trip.

• Travel free as a travel writer. If you like to travel and have a flair for writing, you have a good chance of paying for your travels by selling your experiences, short stories, photos, etc., to publications and newspapers that are looking for a new point of view about a different place. Nearly every mature adult publication and dozens of consumer magazines and newspapers can use feature stories, photo spreads and columns on travel, since it is one of the most popular topics of interest to readers.

• Become an air courier. An air courier is someone who accompanies freight (usually small parcels and envelopes filled with documents), which has been checked as baggage on a flight. In the case of foreign flights, the package arrives with the courier and is processed through customs immediately along with the courier's other bags rather than remaining in a warehouse waiting customs clearance. Courier companies offer assignments to the general public in exchange for free or deeply discounted tickets (50 percent or more). The key to becoming a courier is being flexible and able to travel light. Courier firms want their representatives to maintain a well-dressed, respectable image and welcome responsible mature people they can rely on.

• Buy a new automobile overseas. Several European delivery specialists will pay your round-trip airfare if you buy an automobile from and pick it up overseas. They also arrange necessary customs and vehicle inspections once the car arrives in the United States. You can save from $4,000 to $7,000 on a new Jaguar, BMW, Mercedes, Volvo, Saab, Porsche, Audi, Volkswagen, etc., by arranging European delivery.

- Become a lecturer, performer, or organizer aboard a cruise ship. You can cruise free as an expert on a specific subject, business, or other interesting field. Historians, anthropologists, financial experts, naturalists, former athletes, coaches, musicians, cosmetologists, writers, entertainers, retired executives, CEOs, teachers, etc. are always in high demand to provide guests with an entertaining and interesting array of information and activities. Your job would be to present a series of lectures, organize activities, etc., and be available for informal demonstrations and discussions. In return you receive an all expenses paid cruise.

Home Exchange

A great way to stretch your travel dollars is to participate in a home exchange program. There are several books, clubs and exchange services that list thousands of homes around the world whose owners offer club members a free stay for a week or more. Intervac, an international home exchange service, publishes two directories a year with more than 11,000 listings and details on how to set up an exchange. More than 80 percent of the listings are from outside the United States, ranging as far away as Brazil, Nepal, Australia and Zimbabwe, but most of the exchange homes are in Europe. Subscriptions are $95 per year. For information contact: Intervac, 800-756-4663. Web site: http:// intervac-online.com. E-mail: info@intervacusa.com.

Home Base Holidays www.homebase-hols.com. Operated in an alliance of established home exchange agencies worldwide to ensure members have a wide choice of quality listings in several countries.

HomeLink www.homelink.org is the world's largest home exchange club with 72 countries and web sites in 17 languages.

Vacation Homes Unlimited www.exchangehomes. com offers home exchange listings to members.

House-Sitting

If you like the idea of a free place to stay, consider becoming a professional house-sitter. This is one way to enjoy beautifully furnished (sometimes including maid-service) homes and mansions for free. Most people would rather not abandon their pets to a strange kennel or leave their houses vacant while they travel. A professional house-sitter can spend nearly all year helping different folks out by watching their houses and pets, usually getting paid for it. Free house-sitting works in the opposite way as well. People who own expensive vacation and resort homes often visit these homes only once or twice a year. They also want the peace of mind of having their homes watched over and cared for while they are not there. When they arrive for their vacation, you can visit friends or relatives while they are vacationing in "your" home. How does year-round living in Key West, Florida; Kannapali Beach, Maui; Aspen, Colorado or Malibu, California sound? Many people have homes in the Bahamas, Mexico and other foreign countries that they prefer to have lived in year-round.

Another way to live and travel for free is by house-sitting for homes that are for sale. Houses built for "spec" and model homes especially are perfect for house-sitting. Higher priced homes often stay on the market for several months at a time. Meanwhile, you are enjoying a brand new home. Older homes up for sale are often left empty because their owners have already moved into new homes. Fine homes with swimming pools, tennis courts and lush gardens need someone to watch over them so vandals don't take advantage of their being empty for long periods of time.

Planning Trips and Using Travel Agencies

The simplest and best place to start planning a trip is with a professional travel agency. Choose one that is a member of the American Society of Travel Agents (ASTA) www.astanet.com. Most services and counseling provided by travel agents is free of charge. Agents make their money from commissions paid by airlines or other travel businesses.

You can choose a travel agency that specializes in a particular type of travel or travel to a specific geographic area. There are agencies that specialize in cruises, general pleasure travel, or business travel. Some handle groups and tours while others work only with individual travelers.

ASTA has senior memberships, for those travel professionals who have been an ASTA member (with ASTA membership in their name) for more than 12 years. For more information contact ASTA at: 1101 King St., Ste. 200, Alexandria, VA 22314. E-mail: join@astahq.com.

Ask yourself these questions when choosing a travel agent:

- Are your personal travel requests considered by the agent, such as first- or ground-floor accommodations, in-room amenities, smoking or non-smoking seats and hotel rooms, and bellman to carry heavy luggage?
- When discussing budgets, are you asked about your flexibility in making travel arrangements?
- Are you asked about health concerns?
- Will your travel agent follow through on your behalf, especially if a problem arises during your trip?

If the answers to these questions are "yes," then you have found a good agency for your travel plans.

You can help your agent by making a list of the kinds of activities, recreation, and accommodations you prefer. Also make a rough budget of what you expect to spend and save. If you hate traveling in groups or you don't want to spend more than $60 for dinner, or you prefer to shop rather than sightsee, list those desires as well. Take travel brochures from the agency to help you. Travel agents can advance-book everything from hotel reservations and transportation, to theater tickets and dinner reservations. Working closely with them will assure you of a smooth-running, well-planned trip.

Should you plan your trip yourself? Since fares and rates sometimes change daily, a travel agency's sophisticated computer system linked to thousands of current prices gives them the advantage of having this information at their fingertips. If you are planning a complex trip including many stops, I suggest using a professional travel agent. A recent survey of New York City travel agents showed that prices quoted for the lowest airfare to other cities varied more than 50 percent. Some travel agents quote the first price they see and don't bother to find out about the bargains. This shows how important it is to establish a working relationship with a single travel agent who will be more inclined to spend time on your travel needs.

Contact the following to help in your search:

American Society of Travel Agents (ASTA) www. astanet.com. World Headquarters: 1101 King Street, Suite 200, Alexandria, VA 22314. 703-739-2782 or 800-440-2782. E-mail: join@astahq.com.

Ask if there are any additional charges for arranging a trip. Some agencies bill clients for long distance phone calls, faxes, or other services. Also, always ask about any restrictions or cancellation fees which may apply to your tickets or reservations. Finally, be sure to let your agent know from the beginning that you are a mature adult and, as such, are entitled to all senior discounts available.

Doing It Yourself

If you decide to plan your own trip always ask for the "senior citizen discount" when making your reservations, at the time of purchase or before you check-in. If you wait until you pick up your tickets or check out, it might be too late. Some hotels do not give a senior citizen discount if reservations are booked through a travel agent because they are paying two discounts, a 10 percent travel agent's commission and a 10 percent (or more) senior citizen discount. Also, be aware that you can save money by using toll-free numbers to reserve hotel rooms in hundreds of destinations. Call 800-555-1212 to obtain toll-free numbers.

Some discounts may apply only between certain hours, on certain days of the week, or during specific seasons of the year. Check this out before making reservations.

Don't always take the over-50 discount without inquiring about other available rates. Sometimes special promotional discounts, available to anybody at any age, turn out to have better savings. Ask the reservationist or ticket seller to find you the lowest possible rate at that time.

Since many mature adults look younger than their chronological age, it is particularly important to carry identification with your proof of age (driver's license, passport, resident alien card, Medicare card, senior I.D. card, birth certificate) or proof of membership in an over-50 organization such as AARP.

If you want to try your luck with online booking and auctions look up these sites and compare their different programs, pricing structure and ease of use:

Bid4Travel www.bid4travel.com.

EBay www.ebay.com.

Expedia www.expedia.com.

Generous Adventures Travel Auctions www.gener ousadventures.com.

Luxury Link www.luxurylink.com.

PriceLine http://travel.priceline.com.

SkyAuction.com www.skyauction.com.

Travel.com www.travel.com.

Travelocity www.travelocity.com.

Travelzoo www.travelzoo.com.

Cheap Tickets www.cheaptickets.com. Cheap tick-ets started as America's travel store in 1986. They specialize in low fare and discount airline tickets and provide millions of discount tickets. Their tickets are for regularly scheduled flights, out of all major airports in the United States, Europe, Asia and South America, and on all major airlines. Now you can search for cheap tickets online, 24 hours a day. The search is free to registered users.

Travel Agencies, Clubs and Organizations for 50+ Travelers

Some travel agencies and organizations cater solely to mature travelers. They offer trips and vacations for the fiercely independent or those who enjoy the companionship of tour groups. There are so many choices for the mature traveler today that the only problem is making a decision on where to go.

Tip: Remember to check your tour brochure carefully to see whether tipping for local guides and bus drivers is included in the cost of your vacation package. It is customary to tip the tour director at the end of your tour. Depending on the person's performance, $1–$3 per day per traveler is sufficient.

Experienced Travel Companies

Cruises Inc. http://rloiselle.cruisesinc.com. 1415 NW 62nd Street, Fort Lauderdale, FL 33309. 800-854-0500.

The Cruise Marketplace www.cruisemarketplace.com. 530 El Camino Real, San Carlos, CA 94070. 800-826-4333.

Grand Circle Travel www.gct.com. Grand Circle Travel, Inc., 347 Congress St., Boston, MA 02210. 617-350-7500; 800-959-0405, is the oldest of the U.S. firms dealing only with senior citizens (quarterly magazine, Pen Pal, and travel-partner service). In business for more than 40 years, it enjoys a large and loyal following who respond especially to offers of extended-stay vacations in off-season months, and to low-cost foreign areas with mild climates. The greater number of Grand Circle's passengers are those spending 2 to 20 weeks on the Mediterranean coast of Spain, in a seaside kitchenette apartment supplied with utensils, china, and cutlery.

Others go for several weeks to Portugal and Madeira, the Canary Islands, and the Balearics. The tour company states that older Americans can enjoy a "full season" at these exotic locations for not much more than they'd spend to go to Florida or other domestic havens.

While neither Spain nor Portugal offers swimming weather in winter, their low prices enable seniors (even those living mainly on Social Security) to vacation in dignity, enjoying good-quality meals and modern apartments in place of the fast-food outlets and shabby motels to which they're often relegated here at home. Grand Circle's extended stays are supplemented by nearly a dozen other programs: Alaskan cruises, European and Asian River cruises, hiking and biking holidays, Canadian holidays, inexpensive homestays, tours to Europe, India, Africa and the Orient. These options, though booked by thousands, are not yet as popular as those "stay-put" vacations of several weeks in a balmy, foreign clime.

The Alternatives to Solitude

If you are a mature single, you don't have to travel alone. Grand Circle Travel, Inc. offers a Roomate Finding Service for seniors traveling alone. See their web site at www.gct.com.

Elderhostel. 11 Avenue de Lafayette, Boston, MA 02111. 617-426-7788. Elderhostel is the much-discussed, increasingly popular nonprofit group that works with 2,000 U.S. and foreign educational institutions to provide seniors 55 and over with residential study courses at unbeatable costs: as low as $496 per week for room, board, and instruction and field trips (but not including air fare) in the U.S.; an average of $5,000 for three weeks abroad, this time including air fare. Accommodations and meals are in student residence halls, underused youth hostels or standard motels and hotels. Web site: www.elderhostel.org.

Connecting: Solo Travel Network. 689 Park Road, Unit 6, Gibsons, BC V0N 1V7 Canada. 604-886-9099. This Canadian company offers a bimonthly 20-page newsletter full of information and tips for the solo traveler. Web site: www.cstn.org.

Mayflower Tours. 1225 Warren Avenue, P.O. Box 490, Downers Grove, IL 60515. 630-435-8500, 800-323-7604. Mayflower targets mature travelers 55 or over by offering leisurely paced, fully escorted trips including tours to Hawaii, the Canadian Rockies, and Georgia's Golden Isles. Special trips allow grandparents and grandchildren to travel together. Participants travel by air conditioned motorcoach, stay in quality hotels, and eat meals with others in the tour. If you are a single traveler, Mayflower will find you a roommate as long as you make your reservations 30 days in advance. Web site: www.mayflowertours.com.

Vantage Deluxe World Travel. www.vantagetravel.com. 90 Canal Street, Boston, MA 02114-2031. 617-878-6014 or toll free 800-322-6677 outside Massachusetts.

Vantage sends over 400,000 senior citizens on vacation each year. Vantage creates upscale, escorted tours on both land and sea to destinations all over the world, including Canada, Europe, Russia, China, Latin America, even Iceland. Prices on all tours include airfare, several meals, lodging at four- and five-star hotels, and all of the sightseeing on the tour.

Among Vantage's most popular programs are river cruises in Europe: offered year round on any of Vantage's three luxury river cruise ships, which sail the Rhine, Danube, and Maine rivers. Vantage also offers great prices on several of the world's top ocean cruise lines, including Cunard, Holland America, and Norwegian Cruise Lines. The Cultural Connection series of tours allows seniors to go "behind the scenes" in the countries they visit, experiencing lectures, special meals, "hands-on" participation in local activities, home visits, receptions, and performances.

Vantage specializes in making travel plans for people over 50. Trips can be booked by telephone using the toll free Reservations number: 800-322-6677. For single travelers, Vantage provides a roommate-matching program. A SmartPay Discount Plan allows seniors to save up to 10 percent by paying for trips early. Vantage also offers other ways to receive travel discounts, including their frequent traveler program, the President's Club, and discounts for first-time travelers.

O Solo Mio. 160 Main Street, Los Altos, CA 94022. 800-959-8568. Geared to single mature audiences. Roommate matching service.

YMT Vacations, Inc. ("Your Man Tours"). 8831 Aviation Boulevard, Inglewood, California 90301. 800-922-9000; 310-649-3820; fax: 310-649-2118. Web site: www.ymtvacations.com. YMT, 40 years in business, operates almost solely in the United States, though it has recently branched out with tours to the Caribbean, Panama Canal, and Europe. Its tours are fully escorted, and sometimes consist of a mixture of tour modes: a one-week stay in an attractive land location followed by a one-week cruise; a tour by air to all four of the major Hawaiian Islands (from $1600 plus air fare); a cruise of Alaskan waters, followed by a land tour of Alaska. Of all the senior citizen specialists, YMT is perhaps the least expensive; it offers excellent values, and takes pleasure in attracting cost-conscious seniors to its fully escorted arrangements.

AARP Travel Service. 601 E St NW, Washington DC 20049. 800-303-4222. AARP members have a variety of travel benefits from which to choose. Including escorted tours, trips and cruises to locations all over the globe at discounted group rates. Memberships in AARP cost $12.50/year and includes the monthly publications *AARP The Magazine* and the *AARP Bulletin*. Minimum age is 50. If you belong to an organization like AARP, some of these bargains are yours at age 50. Others come along a little later at varying birthdays, so watch for the cutoff points. In many cases, if the person purchasing the ticket qualifies for the minimum age requirement, others sharing the same accommodations are entitled to the same reduced rates. Web site: www.aarp.org. Email: member@aarp.org.

The Travel Companion Exchange. P.O. Box 833, Amityville, NY 11701. For information call: 631-454-0880.

Where to Stay: Hotel, Motel and Resort Bargains

Today's mature traveler has more choices of accommodations than ever before. Almost anywhere you go you will find a senior discount. Whether you make reservations yourself or through a travel agent, consider the following:

- Hotels, motels, and resorts often offer even better discounts if you belong to a recognized senior organization or discount airline program. Remember to ask at what age the senior discount begins.

- When calling for reservations know the dates, arrival time, number of people in your party, price range, type and quality of room you prefer (including amenities and extras such as nonsmoking rooms, free complimentary breakfasts, health &

fitness centers, indoor pools and Jacuzzis, facilities for the handicapped, etc.)

• Whenever possible use (800) toll-free numbers to book reservations through a central operator.

• Always ask about the senior citizen discount at the time you make reservations and when you check-in. Hotel/motel discounts range from 10 percent to as high as 50 percent off regular room rates.

• Request a written confirmation or a reservation confirmation number and bring it when you check in. Also consider guaranteeing your reservation by prepaying the first night (either by credit card or check). By doing this, whether you use it or not, you are guaranteed a reservation that will be held for you even if you arrive late.

• Another way to guarantee your reservation is to prepay through a travel voucher from your travel agent. Visa, MasterCard, and other major credit card companies now issue these through travel agents. To use a travel voucher, simply present it when you check in.

Accommodations for today's mature traveler run the range of price and comfort levels. Prices range from $15 up to several hundred dollars a night depending on your preferences. Listed below are examples of national and international lodging organizations offering senior discounts:

Baymont Inns www.baymontinns.com. This inexpensive motel chain offers a 10 percent discount in many of its establishments, if you are 60 or over. Baymont Inns are located in about 33 states with over 170 locations. Confirm your discount when making reservations. Call 877-229-6668.

Best Western www.bestwestern.com. Best Western has more than 3,300 independently owned hotels, inns and resorts across the United States and abroad. Most of the affiliates offer a 10 percent senior discount if you are 55 or over. AARP members receive a 10 percent discount on room rates. Advance reservations are recommended. Call 800-780-7234.

Budget Host Inns www.budgethost.com. Located across the United States and Canada, this chain of inns offers senior citizen discounts that vary from inn to inn. There is an abundance of information about their locations, discounts, services, etc. online at the web site. Or you can write them at: P.O. Box 14341, Arlington, TX 76094 or call toll free: 800-283-4678.

Country Hearth Inns www.countryhearth.com. A chain of inexpensive motels that offer a 10 percent discount if you are over 50. Over 60 locations. Call 888-4-HEARTH. E-mail: info@countryhearth.com.

Days Inns www.daysinn.com. From 10% to 50% (usually 10%) off at 1,800 participating inns, hotels, and suite-hotels in the United States, Canada, Mexico, the Netherlands, and France. They also feature "Day Stops" for members (50 years and older) of their September Days Club; as well as 10% off meals, and discounts on Alamo Car rentals. September Days members are entitled to group rates on trips and escorted tours, discounted prescription drugs, vehicle insurance plans, discounts at theme parks, free luggage tags, and information on last-minute travel opportunities. 800-329-7466.

Drury Hotels www.druryhotels.com. If you are over 50 or a member of AARP, Drury Hotels offer 10 percent discounts on regular rooms at all locations. Call 1-800-DRURYINN.

Embassy Suites Hotels www.embassy-suites.com. Discounts vary for each Embassy hotel. Complimentary breakfast and cocktails are also included. Call 800-EMBASSY (362-2779).

Exel Inns Of America, Inc. www.exelinns.com. Located in Michigan, Illinois, Texas, Wisconsin, Minnesota and Iowa, these inns offer a 10 percent senior citizen discount on room rates if you are 55 or over. Call 800-367-3935.

Fairmont Hotels (formerly known as Canadian Pacific) www.fairmont.com. Offers special senior citizen discounts at participating hotels. There are 37 locations through the United States and Canada with many historic luxury properties. They also offer special weekend rates. Call 800-257-7544.

Hampton Inns www.hampton-inn.com (a part of the Hilton). AARP members get a 10 percent discount. The discount is honored at all of the 220 Hampton Inns across the United States. Call 800-HAMPTON (426-7866).

Holiday Inns and Holiday Inn Crowne Plaza Hotels www.sixcontinentshotels.com. Guests 55 and over or members of AARP receive a 10 percent discount on all room rates at over 1,000 participating hotels. Call 877-424-2449.

Howard Johnson www.howardjohnson.com. Take 10% off for both seniors 60 years and older and AARP members, at all of the nation's H.J. hotels. Phone toll free: 800-446-4656.

Hyatt Hotels www.hyatt.com. Age does have its privileges. If you are 62 or over, you are eligible to save up to 50% off their regular room rates at participating Hyatt hotels and resorts in the continental United States and Canada. In addition, be sure to take advantage of Gold Passport, Hyatt's award-winning frequent guest program. As a Gold Passport member, you can choose to earn either Gold Passport points or airline miles on every stay. Your points can be redeemed for exciting travel awards such as room upgrades, nights at Hyatt or even complete vacations! Plus, on every stay, you will receive membership benefits. To join Gold Passport, visit http://goldpassport.hyatt.com. For more information, call 888-591-1234.

Knights Inn www.knightsinn.com. A guaranteed 10% discount to persons 60 and over and AARP members—sometimes it's more than 10%. 250 locations across the United States and Canada. Call 800-843-5644.

La Quinta Inns www.lq.com. Offers up to 30% off to people age 55 and older and to AARP members. Call 800-642-4241.

Marriott Hotels www.marriotthotels.com. At more than 2,000 Marriotts in the United States, seniors 62 and over receive 15% off normal rates. Seniors 62+ also receive 15% off at Marriott's Fairfield Inns and Courtyards by Marriott (two subsidiary chains) and at Marriott's Residence Inns. Phone Marriott at 888-236-2427, Courtyard by Marriott at 800-321-2211, Residence Inn at 800-331-3131, and Fairfield Inns at 800-228-2800.

Omni Hotels www.omnihotels.com. Fifty locations in the United States offer 10 percent discount on regular room rates to seniors 55 and over. Advance reservations suggested. Call 888-444-6664.

Peabody Hotels www.peabodyorlando.com, www. peabodymemphis.com, www.peabodylittlerock.com. The Orlando Peabody offers up to 50% off the starting rate, depending on room availability for seniors, with some rates starting at $160. You can also earn United Airline Miles for your stay. Three locations: Orlando, Florida; Little Rock, Arkansas; and Memphis, Tennessee.

The Pointe Hilton Resorts. These two resorts in Phoenix offer AARP discounts to guests 50 or over. Locations are in Tapatio Cliff and Squaw Peak. Call 800-685-0550.

Quality Inns/Comfort Inns/Clarion (Choice Hotels International) www.choicehotels.com. With over 3,000 hotels worldwide, Choice Hotels International offers year round senior rate programs. If you are 60+, you are eligible for the Super Saver rate of 20 to 30 percent off the room rate and some services. If you are a member of AARP you get a 15 percent off rate, and if you are 50+ you get a 10 percent off rate. Call 877-424-6423.

Radisson www.radisson.com. There are 345 locations in 39 countries. They offer a Goldpoints Plus program that any age person can join. For more information, call 888-201-1718.

Ramada Inns www.ramada.com. Many (about three-quarters) give the same 10% off to persons 60 and up and AARP members. Phone toll free 800-272-6232.

Red Lion Hotels and West Coast Hotels http://red lion.rdln.com, http://westcoast.rdln.com. Both senior citizens 50 and over and AARP members receive a 10 percent discount off the room rates. Please call 800-325-4000 for West Coast reservations; 800-RED-LION for reservations at Red Lion Hotels.

Red Roof Inns www.redroof.com. Offers a savings program called "RediCard" which entitles members to a 10 percent discount on room rates, plus discounts on future stays at Red Roof Inns. Good at over 300 locations across the United States, the RediCard also gives first preference to those applying for nonsmoking rooms. Even if you don't sign up for the RediCard, all seniors 60 and over receive a 10 percent discount on room rates. Call 800-733-7663.

Sheraton Hotels/Starwood Resorts www.starwood hotels.com/sheraton. Located in over 62 countries, participating Sheraton Hotels offer the standard AARP discount to those over 60. Ask for the discount when making reservations. Though they caution that the discount can be withheld during periods of peak business, and is not applicable to minimum-rate rooms, virtually all Sheratons give up to a 50% discount to persons 60 and older. Phone toll free 800-325-3535.

Sonesta International Hotels www.sonesta.com. If you are a member of AARP, you will receive a 10 to 15 percent discount off room rates at any of their 13 deluxe hotels. Make sure to request your discount when making reservations. Call 1-800-SONESTA.

Super 8 Motels, Inc. www.super8.com. Over 1,900 Super 8 Motels across the United States and Canada can offer up to a 10 percent discount for AARP members and seniors 60 or over. Rates vary from hotel to hotel. Call 800-800-8000.

Travelodge and Discount Hotels www.travelodge.com. Participating locations offer a 10 percent discount on room rates to members of most senior organizations. Over 300 locations. For more savings join Travelodge's TripRewards program. For more information visit www.triprewards.com. Call 800-578-7878.

Vagabond Inns www.vagabondinns.com. AARP rates vary from 10% to 30% depending on location. Forty-two locations in California, two in Nevada, one in New Mexico.

Westin Hotels and Resorts www.starwoodhotels.com/westin. This luxury hotel chain offers discounts up to 50 percent off regular room rates. Advance reservations are required. Each hotel has its own discount policy.

Tip: Always check for a senior citizen discount, even if you are booking into an independently owned establishment. You have nothing to lose by asking, and you may find they offer considerable savings in order to stay competitive with the chain operators.

If You Don't Want to Stay in a Hotel

If you are innovative, imaginative and will consider alternative sources of lodging, the following possibilities can also save you money in your travels.

Two resources to assist you in alternate sources of travel are: www.stay4free.com and www.travelsecrets.com.

INNter Lodging. INNter Lodging is a co-op organization. Members stay in a choice of homes across the United States and Canada at very little cost. Members must agree to make their homes available to other travelers at least four months of the year. For information write to INNter Lodging Co-op, 1722 N. Lexington Street, Tacoma, Washington 98406; or call 253-756-0343.

Servas www.servas.org. 1125 16th St., Suite 201, Arcata, CA 95521. 707-825-1714. E-mail: helpdesk@ servas.org. SERVAS is an agency that promotes a more people-friendly form of lodging. Staying with families while abroad serves the triple purpose of avoiding loneliness, gaining new friendships and insights, and lowering costs. You not only escape from that burdensome single supplement, but start from a radically lower base of costs.

On the eve of a trip, members obtain from Servas the names and addresses of families in every major city who have expressed their willingness to receive other Servas members into their homes (for short stays) free of charge, because they believe in the profound moral aspect of such hospitality. Yearly fee for Servas membership: $85—not including $25 refundable deposit.

Women Welcome Women www.womenwelcome women.org.uk. 88 Easton Street, High Wycombe,

Buckinghamshire, HP11 1LT, United Kingdom. Or call 011-44-1494-465441, between 9:30am and 1:30 P.M. (British time). 2,500 members strong, currently in its 19th year of operation. This club was formed to facilitate "cultural exchanges" between women from all parts of the globe. The club also arranges conferences and gatherings where members take courses, hear lectures, sightsee and socialize in the home city of the sponsoring member.

Regular homestays are arranged on a person-to-person basis. A member looks through the organization's directory (sent out annually, it includes the names and addresses of all members), decides where they want to travel, and then contacts members in the area to see if they can accommodate them. W.W.W. currently has members in 82 countries, including such exotic locales as Vietnam, Turkey, Zimbabwe, Kazakhstan, and Latvia. There are high concentrations in Europe (particularly Germany, the U.K., the Netherlands, Belgium and Switzerland), Australia, Japan and the U.S. The suggested donation for membership is 35 British pounds (approximately $60 to $70) to defray their cost.

YMCA www.ymca.net. The YMCA offers inexpensive accommodations throughout North America that are safe, comfortable, and conveniently located. You should make reservations several months in advance due to their popularity. Included is your room, use of swimming pool, exercise facilities, and library. Some Y's offer package programs that include breakfast, some other meals, and sightseeing. Write: YMCA, 101 North

Wacker Drive, Chicago, Illinois 60606. Call 312-977-0031 to find the YMCA nearest your location.

Auto-Truck Stops. Full-service truck stops offer inexpensive, comfortable hotel rooms. Some include amenities such as laundromats, restaurants, barbershops, and convenience stores. First priority for available rooms is reserved for truckers.

Campus Accommodations. Colleges and universities across the United States, Canada, and Europe rent rooms to travelers in the summertime and during school vacations. The cost is minimal, and some include breakfast and use of campus facilities. Contact the housing office of colleges in areas you plan to visit or get a copy of *U.S. and Worldwide Travel Accommodations Guide*. Check for a copy of the *Campus Lodging Guide* by B&J Publications at your local library. It is no longer in print, but is very helpful in locating campus accommodations.

Oakwood Resort Apartments. Oakwood Corporate Housing Resort Apartments www.oakwood.com. These resort apartments may be rented by mature travelers 55 and over. They are located in metropolitan areas in California, Nevada, Washington DC, Georgia, Virginia, North Carolina, Texas, and Colorado. They must be rented for 30 days or more, and if rented between November and February, there is a substantial discount. The apartments are completely furnished, including kitchen utensils, and linens. Most locations have tennis courts, fitness centers, swimming pools, and clubhouses. Write to: Oakwood Worldwide, 2222 Corinth Ave., Los Angeles, CA 90064, or call 877-902-0832.

Camping

According to a survey by the camping industry, the number of campers who are retirees is increasing. And as that number continues to grow, the over-50 crowd will be requiring more conveniences and a greater choice of recreational activities. There are public campgrounds, private campgrounds, primitive camp-grounds, and luxurious resort campgrounds. Many are located near historic points of interest, major attractions or within state and national parks. Prices range from as low as $1.50 to $20 per night. Amenities include fire-places, picnic tables, flush toilets, showers, electricity, running water, grocery stores, dumping stations, and coin laundries. For information about the National Park System—including Annual Passes, Senior Passes, and Access Passes—see the last section of this chapter.

Kampgrounds of America (KOA) www.koakamp grounds.com is the largest chain of privately owned campgrounds in the U.S. For information send for the KOA Directory. Kampgrounds are located in the United States and Canada. Write: Kampgrounds of America, P.O. Box 30558, Billings, MT 59114; 406-248-7444, or pick up a directory at your nearest KOA campground.

Another multi-site campground operation is Yogi Bear's Jellystone Park Camp Resorts and Safari Campground http://campjellystone.com in New Hampshire. Call 800-558-2954. Each campground has different discount policies. Ask when you make your reservations if they have special grandparent rates when you travel with grandchildren.

A highly successful international organization, The Good Sam Club www.goodsamclub.com, offers discounts and benefits to owners of recreational vehicles. Although membership is open to all ages, the majority of those belonging are over 50. Over 2,000 local chapters host outings, hold meetings and schedule regular campouts. Savings and services include: 10 percent discount at 1,700 RV parks and campgrounds; 10 percent discounts on RV parts and accessories; Emergency road service (includes towing); RV vehicle insurance; Health insurance; Subscriptions to Highways magazine; Trip routing service; Mail forwarding service; Credit card protection; Lost pet service and lost key service. With all these benefits and a membership fee of $19 a year, The Good Sam Club is a bargain for folks who spend a lot of time on the road. They also organize "caraventure" tours all over the world. For information call 1-800-234-3450 or go on to their web site.

RVing Women www.rvingwomen.com. P.O. Box 1940, Apache Junction, AZ 85217. 888-55-RVING or 480-671-6226. E-mail: rvingwomen@juno.com. Offers advice, support, seminars, caravans, and a bi-monthly magazine and membership directory to "on-your-own" women RV'ers who are single, widowed, divorced or have husbands who just hate camping. Membership is $45 a year.

Bed and Breakfasts

There are so many wonderful bed & breakfast accommodations located in the United States and abroad that it would be impossible to try and list them. For the most current information regarding bed and breakfast establishments in areas you plan to visit, contact the tourist agencies in those areas or check your local bookstore or library for bed and breakfast directories. The AAA Club Directory for each state also lists and rates bed and breakfasts.

Evergreen Club www.evergreen club.com. P.O. Box 194, Franklin Grove, IL 61031. 815-456-3111. E-mail: info@evergreenclub.com. The Evergreen Club is designed for those mature travelers over 50 willing to give up rooms in their homes to other travelers. Club members provide guest rooms for fellow members traveling throughout the United States, Canada, and Europe. There are presently over 2,000 homes in the Evergreen Club. Membership costs $75 per couple or $60 for singles. Members receive annual directories and a quarterly newsletter. The directory gives names, addresses, occupations, interests, policies on smoking and pets and a listing of special attractions in the area. Rates are $15 a night for two, $10 for one person.

More Clubs for Mature Travelers

Partners-In-Travel www.partners-in-travel.com. 1407 W. Prien Lake Road, Holly Hill Plaza, Lake Charles, LA 70601. 337-480-0246. E-mail: info@partners-in-travel.com. Partners-in-Travel, open to all ages, offers single travelers an opportunity to connect with other travelers for friendship and savings on the cost of travel.

Loners on Wheels www.lonersonwheels.com. P.O. Box 1060-WB, Cape Girardeau, MO 63702. 866-LOW-CLUB. E-mail: lonersreply@clas.net. Operates for mature singles with recreational vehicles. A rather large organization, it forms caravans of RVs operated solely by singles, and takes them to rallies and camp-outs all over the country and occasionally to Mexico. Annual dues: $45.

Escapees RV Club www.escapees.com. 100 Rainbow Drive, Livingston, TX 77351. 888-757-2582. Escapees is a club and support network for RVers. There are more than 34,000 members throughout the country. They hold campouts, meetings, rallies, and caravans all over the country. Members receive an annual travel guide and directory and the *Escapees* Magazine detailing events and activities. Annual member fee is $60, with a one-time $10 enrollment fee for new members.

Travel Companion Exchange www.travelcompanions.com. P.O. Box 833, Amityville, NY 11701. 631-454-0880. This organization was founded by the well-known travel figure, Jens Jurgen. His is the most elaborate of all travel match-up services, supplying you with literally thousands of available listings, all carefully grouped by computer into helpful categories ("special interests," "special travel plans," and the like) to enable you to make a wise choice. You will find a suitable travel "match-up." Annual fee is $298.

American Jewish Congress International Travel Program www.ajcongresstravel.com. 15 E. 84th Street, New York, NY 10028. 800-221-4694; 212-879-4500. This organization offers tours with Jewish themes to Israel and several other international locations. They have a roommate-matching service for single travelers.

Fly and Save Money

Most airlines offer senior citizens discounts of at least 10 percent off regular fares (you can fly first class for free if you can prove you are 100 years old!). However, these fares often cost more than if you used excursion fares, also referred to as Supersaver, MaxSaver, and UltraSaver fares, where the discount may be 50 percent or more. Often "limited time only" promotional fares offer even more savings (up to 80 percent) at certain times when airlines are looking to fill seats. There is no difference between the seating, service, or aircraft on a full-coach or economy ticket and an excursion/promotional fare ticket. However, there are usually only a certain number of these cut-price seats available on each flight, so it is important to book as early as possible. In fact, if you are going to use your senior discount with a Supersaver fare, you will most likely be required to make your reservations at least 30 days in advance.

SuperSaver and MaxSaver fares carry a number of important restrictions. There are usually hefty cancellations fees, ticket change fees, blackout periods, a 7- to 30-day cancellation requirement, a 24-hour payment requirement, round-trip purchase requirement, Saturday night stayover, and other conditions. Always ask about all applicable restrictions before purchasing your tickets. You need to decide whether these limitations and inconveniences are worth the savings. If you are flexible in your plans, they usually are.

Airlines currently use three different methods to attract mature travelers:

1. Clubs with discounts (frequent flyers)
2. Straight discounts.
3. Unlimited-mileage passes.

The minimum age for discount senior fares is 50, usually honored in conjunction with proof of membership in AARP. However, check with individual airlines since some offer senior rates starting at age 60 or older. Most programs allow a companion of any age, regardless of sex or relationship to travel at the same reduced fare.

When choosing among the confusing, ever-changing fares airlines offer, always ask for the lowest current fare. Check local newspaper advertisements, travel magazines, or one of the several excellent travel newsletters for the latest promotional offers.

Let the airline know that you qualify for a senior discount, but be aware that you may get a better deal by going with a special promotion or supersaver fare. Sometimes your senior discount can cut these low fares even lower. You may even get lucky and hit a special promotional fare for seniors (these are usually run during off-peak seasons). These fares are often significantly lower than other fares and may be the cheapest way to go.

Most airlines no longer offer coupon books for multiple trips for seniors, they simply offer senior discounts.

Tip: Remember all airlines now require a picture I.D. when you check in. So be prepared to present a valid proof of age with photo and, if applicable, your club/airline membership card.

Tip: Airports can be confusing places for older folks who are not used to the hustle-bustle, strange terminals in strange cities, making connecting flights, etc. Remember, if you are traveling with someone who needs extra care, your airline agent will arrange for a wheelchair or special tram to pick up a passenger. The same goes with dietary restrictions that may require a special meal onboard. Some airlines will even grant permission to take your senior relative to the gate instead of saying goodby at the security checkpoint.

Information about airport facilities for seniors (and disabled travelers), such as pay telephones for hearing-impaired travelers or elevators and bathrooms with handicap facilities, is available on most airline web sites. The Travelers Aid Society (located at most airline hubs) provides attendants to help older people make flight connections.

Airline Discounts

Because of the recent world events and changes within the airlines industry, discounts and special offers are always subject to change and time restrictions. Many airlines have begun discontinuing their senior discount programs, instead concentrating on mileage reward programs and offering special deals to certain parts of the country and the world during specific times of the year. We have given you the most up-to-date information available at the time of printing. Always check with the individual airline for their current discount programs and promotional fares.

American Air Lines. 800-433-7300. American Airlines, American Eagle and American Connection offer senior fares in most domestic markets for seniors 65 and older. For further current information, please call American Airlines Reservations at the above toll free number. Note: American Airlines' SkyCAAre program allows passengers to arrange, at the time of flight booking, for emergency room-trained nurses to accompany them every step of the way. SkyCAAre nurses help with meals and getting around and, in an emergency, can administer medical air. This service often is used for seniors transferring to or from nursing homes, though elderly vacationers traveling with relatives often use it to relieve their companions.

ATA Airlines. www.ata.com. 800-I-FLY-ATA. This airlines advertises great fares for seniors. Senior Sale fares apply for ages 65 and over. Seniors may take along one companion on the same flight at the same low,

Senior Sale fare. Senior Sale fares cannot be combined with any other discount offer or fare including ata.com discounts.

Continental Airlines www.continental.com. 800-523-3273. Continental offers senior fares to selected travel destinations for passengers who are 65 and older. Ask for more details on these fares when you make your reservations, or when you make your booking on www.continental.com. Select the Seniors (age 65 and older) category. Continental also offers some coupons for multiple travel and certificates for lower fares.

Delta Air Lines www.delta-air.com. 800-221-1212. Delta no longer offers specific senior discounts, but they do offer several programs such as "SkyMiles" to accumulate miles, special ski and golf packages, and unique e-mail offers only for subscribers to their e-mail newsletter.

Northwest Airlines www.nwa.com. 800-225-2525. Northwest no longer has specific senior fares, but they offer a variety of special offers like companion fares, great deals to Hawaii and Europe, and vacation pack-ages. You can also sign up for "WorldPerks" if you travel frequently. You'll earn miles and points to spend on a wide assortment of travel and gifts.

United Airlines www.united.com. 800-864-8331. Travelers 65 or over can receive discounts on United Airlines flights. They also feature a variety of special deals on domestic and international flights. United has its own frequent flyer program, Mileage Plus, whose members can earn frequent flyer miles for a wide range of activities, from flying on any of United's global partner airlines to dining certificates and downloading music.

There are also special offers from United's partner airlines including Air Canada, Air New Zealand, and Lufthansa. A 50% room-rate discount from participating Hilton Hotels and resorts, Westin Hotels and Resorts, Sheraton Hotels and Resorts, and members of The Luxury Collection, including more than 15 exceptional properties in Hawaii. Members can also redeem and/or earn miles for magazine or newspaper subscriptions, retail services, grocery shopping, and communication devices.

Members also receive bonuses, upgrades and discounts from car rental companies Hertz, Avis, National, and Alamo.

US Airways www.usairways.com. 800-428-4322. US Airways offers seniors 65 and over special senior fares for leisure travel within the United States including roundtrip travel from the U.S. to Canada. There are also special senior rates for those 55 and over on US Airways' partners, such as the major cruise lines Celebrity Cruises, Crystal Cruises, Norwegian Cruise Line, Princess Cruises, Royal Caribbean, Seabourn Cruise Line, and Windstar Cruises.

U.S. Regional Airlines

Alaska Airlines www.alaskaair.com. 800-ALASKA-AIR (1-800-252-7522). Alaska Airlines no longer offers a senior discount, but they do offer a mileage plan for frequent flyers and web specials. If you are a new Alaska Airlines customer, you can also sign up and receive bonus miles in your account.

Aloha Airlines www.alohaairlines.com. 800-367-5250. They have merged with Hawaiian Air. They no longer offer senior discounts, but do offer the "Aloha-Pass" for frequent flyers, and a 7-day Island Pass that will allow you to travel between all the Hawaiian Islands for one fixed price.

Midwest/Skyway Airlines www.midwestexpress.com. 800-452-2022. While Midwest Airlines and Skyline Airlines no longer offer senior discount programs, their frequent flyer program is one of the most rewarding programs in the industry. This program offers special fares, extended stays and more.

Southwest Airlines www.southwestairlines.com. 800-435-9792. Travelers 65 and over receive special senior discounts. Travelers may get details on fares, limitations, and any restrictions from a Southwest Airlines Reservations Sales Agent or a travel agent. Fares are subject to change until tickets are purchased, but Senior Fare tickets are fully refundable. There is also a coupon program good for flights to all Southwest destinations. Coupons are valid every day but advance purchase is required. Reservations are necessary. Web site for senior plans: www.southwest.com/travel_cen ter/seniors.html.

Mexican Airlines

Mexicana Airlines www.mexicana.com. 800-380-8781. Seniors 62 and over receive a 10% discount off of most non-promotional flights to and from the U.S.

Canadian Airlines

Air Canada www.aeroplan.com. 800-361-5373. Air Canada no longer offers senior discounts, but offers "Aeroplan," a frequent flyer program with special rates, vacation packages and more.

European Airlines

Alitalia www.alitaliausa.com. Alitalia is a partner with Delta Airlines, so you can earn frequent flyer miles with each airline if you are a member of either of their programs. They no longer offer a senior discount.

British Airways. 800-AIRWAYS. British Airways offers all seniors age 60 and older a 10 percent discount on select World Traveller (economy) airfares and other related benefits. Be sure to inquire at the time of booking since these discounts and benefits will not apply after you have purchased your ticket. This offer is valid for travel from the U.S. only, and must be booked and paid for in the U.S. If you book online, choose the pay offline option and ask your sales agent about the discount when you call to pay offline.

El Al www.elal.com. 800-223-6700 or 212-768-9200 in N.Y. If you are 60 or over, you are eligible for a 10 to 15 percent discount on El Al flights.

KLM Royal Dutch Airlines www.klm.com. They are now a partner with Northwest Airlines and all ticketing in the U.S. is done through the Northwest web site.

Lufthansa www.lufthansa.com. 800-399-LUFT. If you are 62 or over, Lufthansa offers 10 percent discounts on their fares. The senior discount is not available online and must be booked through the Lufthansa reservations office.

TAPAir Portugal www.flytap.com/USA. 800-221-7370. Offers small senior discounts for those over 60 (and their companions) traveling during off-peak times.

Scandanavian Airlines (SAS) www.flysas.com. 800-221-2350. Travelers 65 or over receive a discount on some flights within Sweden and to the U.S. Book by telephone and request the discount.

Most major airline travel clubs (including American, Continental, Northwest, TWA, United, and USAir) offer special savings for mature adults. There is an initiation fee ranging between $50 and $150.

Take a Cruise for Less
How do you like the idea of a traveling resort? You unpack once and the rest of your transportation

plans are taken care of. A recent survey of American travelers found that almost half of all cruise passengers are over 50. Cruise travel opportunities are nearly endless: Caribbean, Mediterranean, Alaska, South Pacific, the Orient, Hawaii, the Mexican Riviera, Baja California, South America, New England, Eastern Canada, Scandinavia, British Isles, the Mississippi and other rivers, England, the wine country of France, and the Rivers of Germany. You can cruise just about anywhere there's enough water for a ship.

Cruises offer some of the best travel bargains available. If you book your trip far in advance (a year or more) or very close to the date of sailing you can save a bundle, 50% or more off the list price. You can also put yourself on "standby" for an upcoming cruise. Check the travel section of your newspaper for advertisements for last-minute cruise travel.

Agencies that specialize in last-minute travel can offer deep discounts. Although they are called "last-minute," several of them will book passengers in advance knowing these huge ships usually have space available. Last Minute Travel Agencies:

Moment's Notice www.moments-notice.com. 888-241-3366.

Vacations To Go www.vacationstogo.com. 800-338-4962.

Last Minute Travel Club www.lastminuteclub.com. 416-449-5400 or 877-970-3500.

You can also save if you book through a cruise discounter. In this case, you should be knowledgeable about individual cruise ships, itineraries, cabin locations, etc. An online listing of cruise specials is offered by Cruises Only (formerly the Cruise Line, Inc.), a Massachusetts-based discount cruise and information center. For information call 800-CRUISES. www.cruises only.com

When planning your cruise, ask for special cruise values during "shoulder" (between high and low season) and "off" seasons. The cruise is the same, but the price is less if you can travel during times when the demand is lower.

Cruise costs vary according to destination. Prices for a cruise include nearly everything: stateroom, lavish meals, entertainment, pool facilities, gymnasium, social programs, some shore tours and other activities. Compare the prices with the prices you are quoted by your travel agent. Your travel agent can also reserve dinner seating, arrange connecting air and ground transportation, suggest and book pre- and post-cruise tours, and advise on passport and visa requirements.

Be sure to research your cruise before you go. Get real-life travel stories and cruise reviews from seniors like yourself. Also try visiting the web site www.cruise opinion.com.

Cruises for Seniors

Looking for a cruise specifically designed for seniors? Try these outfits:

Sea Escape Cruise Lines www.seaescape.com. 877-732-3722. 954-453-3333. This cruise line offers one-day cruises with special discounts for mature travelers 55 years and over. Cruise ships leave from Port Canaveral, Fort Lauderdale, St. Petersburg, Miami, and Tampa. The best discounts are in the early summer months between April and June. Sea Escape offers seniors up to 10 percent off regular prices.

Cruise One www.cruiseone.com. This cruise line specializes in trips to the Far East, Alaska, Europe, Caribbean, Mexico, South Pacific, Panama Canal, and South America with special reduced rates. Senior travelers receive additional savings. Choose your state for your local cruise representative, who can tell you about current rates and specials.

Special Interest Cruises

One of the most interesting concepts in cruises is the "educational" or "special interest" cruise. These cruises offer high-I.Q. itineraries for people who like the convenience of cruising, but want a vacation with more mental stimulation than shipboard bingo, shopping, and shore excursions. These innovative travel programs are offered by cruise lines, museums, university alumni associations, special interest magazines and other groups. They feature lecturers, expedition leaders and naturalists who are experts in their fields of interest. Some programs are on expedition ships especially designed to reach remote destinations.

Nonprofit groups and cruise companies that sponsor "special interest" cruises:

Abercrombie & Kent International Cruises www.abercrombiekent.com. 800-554-7016

American Museum of Natural History www.amnh.org. 800-462-8687.

Captain Cook's. 800-800-2784.

National Audubon Society http://travel.audubon.org. 212-979-3000.

Smithsonian National Associate Program www.si.edu. 877-EDU-TOUR; 202-357-4700.

Stanford Alumni Association www.stanfordalumni.org. 650-725-1093.

World Wildlife Fund Expeditions www.worldwildlife.org. 888-WWF-TOUR (993-8687).

Galapagos Cruises www.galapagos-inc.com. 866-672-4533.

INTRAV's Clipper Cruises. www.intrav.com/our-trips/small-ship. 800-456-8100. E-mail: info@intrav.com.

Swan Hellenic Cruises www.swanhellenic.com. 877-219-4239.

Travel Dynamics International www.traveldynamics international.com. 800-257-5767; 212-517-7555.

Most groups say their typical passengers are seasoned travelers around age 55. Although these types of trips are generally not a bargain, they do offer a stimulating, intellectual atmosphere not usually found aboard typical cruise ships.

Bus and Railroad Excursions

If you prefer to travel by bus or train, consider the following:

Gray Line Tours www.grayline.com. Booking is done online by destination. Gray Line Tours motor coach company operates in cities throughout the United States. It offers 10 percent off half-day and full-day sightseeing tours at participating locations throughout the United States, Canada and Mexico for members of AARP and other senior organizations. To obtain the discount, purchase tour tickets directly from Gray Line and show a valid AARP Membership card. AARP discounts are not available at the following Gray Line locations: Alaska, Banff, Alberta, Chicago, Flagstaff, Jackson Hole, WY, Las Vegas, NV, Savannah, GA, Seattle/Tacoma, WA, and Victoria British Columbia; Whitehouse, Yukon territory and Yellowstone, MT.

Greyhound Lines, Inc. www.greyhound.com. P.O. Box 660362, Dallas, TX 75266-0362. 800-231-2222 or 800-752-4841 (for passengers with disabilities). Seniors 62 and over may still request a 5% discount at a terminal counter on unrestricted passenger fares. Appropriate ID is required. By booking online, passengers can save 10 percent on advertised locations.

Peter Pan Bus Lines www.peterpanbus.com. 800-237-8747. Travelers 62 and older receive a 5 percent discount on one-way and round-trip unrestricted adult fares. Serving over 100 cities, Peter Pan Bus Lines also operates bus tours as well as services such as a shipping and packing express and basic car maintenance services.

For a list of National Tour Association member companies or information about specific motor coach tours look up the NTA at their web site www.ntaon line.com.

Travelers interested in motor coach tours can also check with their local Automobile Club Association office for information.

Amtrak www.amtrak.com. Senior citizens 62 and over and handicapped mature travelers are entitled to a 15 percent discount on Amtrak by presenting appropriate identification. The discounts are not restricted on holidays. Discounts do not apply to first class accommodations or sleeper accommodations. There are no requirements to buy closed-end round-trip tickets. The senior discounts apply to any regular one-way fare of $50 or more, but buying a round-trip ticket is the most economical way to go. There is no charge for stopovers on one-way tickets, but you must report a stopover when making ticket reservations.

Amtrak operates trains and Metroliners that have reserved seating: coach and club car (first class) seats are available on Metroliners, which service most major Atlantic Coast cities and major metropolitan destinations throughout the United States. Sleeping cars are available between long distances. Snack bars are provided on most trains, and on overnight travel there are dining cars serving meals during the day and evening.

Senior citizen discounts do not apply to Auto Train. A 10 percent discount is available to seniors on the North America Rail Pass. Thirty days, two countries, one pass. The North America Rail Pass is the most adventurous and affordable way to see the United States and Canada. For information contact: 800-USA-RAIL or 800-321-8684, or look them up at their web site.

Via Rail www.viarail.ca. 3 Place Ville-Marie, Suite 500, Montreal, Quebec H3B 2C9, Canada. 800-561-3949; 5114-871-6000. Spending a night on board? VIA offers you Sleeper first class, with your own private bedroom or semi-private section, a comfortable bed, and access to a shower. In a sleeping car, the train is more like a cozy hotel! Other conveniences will help make your trip more enjoyable. For example, people with restricted mobility can board the train ahead of others.

If you are over 60, VIA offers you a 10% discount. There's one condition: if you don't look old enough, a member of their personnel might ask for proof of age. If you are planning to travel for several days during a 30-day period, find out about the Canrailpass. As a senior, you'll be entitled to buy a pass at an even lower price. VIA also offers several promotions and special services just for seniors.

Tip: The rest room is in the same car, at the end of the wide aisle. On most long haul trips, you can enjoy a cup of coffee or tea in the Skyline. Several other trains have a restaurant car, where their chef prepares delicious meals with which you can enjoy a fine wine.

Renting a Car

The key to obtaining the best rate when renting a car is to reserve one in advance. When you call about rates or reservations, always have available a valid driver's license, a major credit card, your senior organization's ID number and you own membership card for reference. Never rent a car without getting a discount or a special promotional rate. Always ask for the lowest rate available at that time.

Most major car rental companies have toll-free reservation offices for reserving a car most anywhere in the world. Below are car rental agencies (and their web sites) that offer special senior rates or discounts:

Alamo www.alamo.com. 800-GO-ALAMO. Alamo offers great rates for those 50 years of age and older. Check their specials online or call the toll free number.

Avis www.avis.com. 800-331-1212. Avis offers special car rental discounts of 5 to 10 percent to senior citizens and members of AARP.

Budget/Sears Rent-A-Car www.budget.com. 800-527-0700. Offers daily rental discounts to members of AARP and other senior organizations. Discounts vary depending on day or time of year.

Dollar www.dollar.com. 800-800-3665. Dollar offers a club for members 50 and over, the Silver Dollar Club. It includes: Special car rental rates for adults over 50; unlimited rental car mileage (geographic restrictions may apply); no charge for additional drivers listed on the rental car agreement; and frequent flyer miles or credits with car rental partners Alaska Airlines, Aloha Airlines, America West, American Airlines, Continental Airlines, Delta Air Lines, Hawaiian Airlines, Japan Airlines, Northwest Airlines, Southwest Airlines, United Airlines, and US Airways.

Hertz www.hertz.com. 800-654-3131. Hertz offers a 10% discount on Standard Rates and a 15% discount on Hertz Daily Member Benefit Rates to members of AARP and other participating senior associations.

National www.nationalcar.com. 800-CAR-RENT. National offers special discounts of 5 to 30 percent to members of Northwest Airlines' WorldPerks Program, and AARP. National also offers discounts to seniors 50 and over. To receive the discount, you must call the number for reservations.

Thrifty Rent-A-Car www.thrifty.com. 800-THRIFTY (847-4389). Seniors 55 and over get 5 percent off regular rates. Members of Northwest Airlines' WorldPerks program and Delta Air Lines' SkyMiles program can earn up to quadruple frequent flyer miles with every Thrifty rental.

Group Tour Programs

Tour programs come in many varieties from complete, door to door escorted excursions with everything planned and included, to highly individual programs where you are mostly on your own. Twenty-five years ago the idea of "taking a tour" meant taking a couple of weeks and covering several cities. Some companies still offer these breathless, whirlwind tours, but most are planned for a more relaxing, quality experience and are generally much less frantic. Your travel agent should recommend member tour operators of the National Tour Association (NTA), an organization requiring financial and performance standards of its members.

A tour package generally covers everything, including most meals, transportation, escorts, sightseeing, group parties, etc. You are required to pay for the full tour in advance. Less-structured tours allow for individual travel activities, with airfare, hotel, airport transfers, and some meals, admissions, etc. included in the package. Since professional tour operators deal in large volume bookings at lower rates, the cost for a package tour is usually lower than if you were to pay for the elements separately.

To help you decide on a tour, make a list of your travel likes, dislikes, preferences, etc. Study brochure descriptions, which usually include details of daily itineraries and organized activities. This will aid you in choosing a tour that is right for you, either one that is strictly scheduled, loosely scheduled with lots of free time, or one somewhere in between. Senior citizen discounts offered by tour operators vary by company, season, and other factors. As with all travel arrangements, ask your travel agent if there is a senior citizen discount for the tour you will be taking.

Some companies that focus their tour programs on mature travelers are:

Arthur Frommer's Budget Tours www.frommers. com. They are now a division of John Wiley & Sons. Corporate Headquarters: 111 River Street, Hoboken, NJ 07030. 201-748-6000. E-mail: contactclub@brand direct.com. "Special travelers are those whom the travel industry sometimes regards as 'problems'— elderly singles, teenagers, the disabled, intellectuals, families with very, very small children, single-minded 'special interest' vacationers, persons traveling to attend a funeral, unaccompanied women, unaccompanied men, and more. For each such group, I attempt not simply to supply general advice, but the specific names, addresses and numbers of companies eager to serve them, travel firms that regard other companies' 'problem passengers' as their 'opportunities'"

Pleasant Hawaiian Holidays www.pleasantholi days.com. 2404 Townsgate Road, Westlake Village, CA 91361. 800-742-9244. Pleasant offers the Makua Club for seniors. Participating hotels offer a free room upgrade, and you will also receive free car rental upgrades and gift certificates that can be used towards the purchase of activities and events in Hawaii. Best of all, there are no applications to sign or membership fees to pay, and only one person per room needs to be at least 55.

Grueninger Tours. www.grueningertours.com. This group specializes in senior tours with professional escorts throughout the U.S. and Canada. Address: 201 West 103rd Street, Suite 380, Indianapolis, IN 46290. 317-465-1122 or 800-844-4159.

Tips for Traveling Abroad
Passports

Passports are required for entry into most foreign countries. As of 2008, all Americans re-entering the U.S. from Canada, Mexico, and the Caribbean will be required to show their passport. Make sure yours is up to date; passports issued prior to 1982 are good for 8 years; passports issued after 1983 are good for 10 years. To apply for a passport contact your federal government building information center or the Passport Agency. Also, check with your local U.S. post office or local courthouse.

Apply for a passport two to three months prior to a planned trip, as it can take up to six weeks to process your application. You will need two photographs—one in color and one in black and white-to get your passport.

Currency

Get U.S. denomination travelers' checks through your bank. Traveler's checks are safer than cash, and if you don't use them, they can be used like cash when you get home. Also, you won't have to pay an exchange fee to convert them back, like you do with foreign currency. Exchange most of your currency after you arrive at your destination since exchange rates are usually better in banks abroad. If you wish to exchange tour dollars into foreign currencies before you leave, just exchange enough for incidentals like tips and taxis. Cash personal checks only as you need them. Again this will avoid having to exchange extra foreign currency back into dollars for a fee.

Tip: In order to avoid carrying too much cash, bring an ATM (Automatic Teller Machine) card with you that is on an international world-wide system. Nearly every "Westernized" country in the world has ATM machines on practically every corner. It's a simple way to get as much cash as you need in the currency you need. For example, Spain has more ATMs than any country in the world. They are everywhere, from the smallest villages to large cities.

Vaccinations

In some areas of the world, particularly the tropics, you need certain vaccinations to protect your health. Ask your travel agent or call your state or local health department about required inoculations or vaccinations. Some medications and vaccinations must be taken two to four weeks in advance of travel, so check far enough ahead to be safe.

The National Center for Disease Control <u>www.cdc.gov</u> in Atlanta has a 24-hour hotline with international health requirements and health recommendations for foreign travelers. Call 877-394-8747 for Traveler's Health.

Visas

Similar to passports, visas are international identification cards. Ask your travel agent which countries require visas, or call the embassies of the countries you plan to visit. Visas are issued through the particular country's embassy in Washington, D.C., or the nearest consular office.

Warning: There are some countries for which travel advisories are issued by the State Department because of uncertain or unsafe conditions for American travelers. The State Department maintains an Advisory Hotline, 202-501-4444, which you can call for updated information. You can also check for advisories online at <u>www.travel.state.gov</u>. The Sunday travel section of the newspaper of a large city will also carry briefs about which countries are not recommended for current travel.

Customs

You can bring up to $800 worth of new merchandise into the United States from abroad without paying taxes on it. The next $1,000 worth of goods is generally taxed at a 10 percent rate. The U.S. Customs Service publishes a free booklet "Know Before You Go," explaining all the customs procedures. For a copy write: Department of the Treasury, U.S., Customer Service

Center, 1300 Pennsylvania Avenue NW, Room 3.4A, Washington, DC 20229. Or you can get the booklet online at www.customs.ustreas.gov.

For a list of U.S. State Department publications on travel look up www.travel.state.gov/travel/tips/broch ures/brochures_1231.html.

Tip: Look up the Federal Citizen Information Center web site at www.pueblo.gsa.gov. There are hundreds of free booklets on dozens of subjects published by this department of the government. Click on "Travel" and find the booklets that are of most interest to you. You can also write them at Pueblo, CO 81009 for a complete current catalog.

Traveling with the Grandkids

If you have grandchildren, traveling with them can be inexpensive, educational and can strengthen the bonds between you and your grandchildren. Many folks feel children between 7 and 13 travel best. As for saving money, airlines often offer discounts for children under 12 (as well as special companion fares) and most hotels allow them to stay in the same room with their grandparents at no extra charge. Cruise lines sometimes offer last-minute specials when they are under booked, allowing kids to travel completely free. Travel with one of the groups below and not only see the world, but improve relationships and communication between generations.

Elderhostel www.elderhostel.org/programs/inter generational_default.asp. 11 Avenue de Lafayette, Boston, MA 02111. 800-454-5768. The senior travel organization also offers intergenerational tours to domestic and international locations all year long. Packages include accommodations, most meals, transportation during the program, and cultural events and activities, and range from short trips in the U.S. that cost less than $600 per person to multi-week international tours.

GrandTravel www.grandtrvl.com. 1920 N. Street NW, Suite 200, Washington, D.C. 20036. 800-247-7651 (in Washington, D.C.: 202-785-8901). This organization arranges tours for grandparents and grandchildren. GrandTravel's series of itineraries are scheduled for normal school breaks. They offer 16 tours, including travel to the western states and national parks, Washington, D.C., Alaska, Hawaii, an American Indian country tour, New England, the Soviet Union, Galapagos Islands, China and Japan, Africa, Scandinavia, Holland, England and Scotland, and New Zealand. Tours are developed by educators, psychologists, and leisure counselors and are structured to encompass both informational and recreational aspects. Trips focus on strengthening the bonds between the grandparent and grandchild, but there is plenty of time for everyone to be with people their own age.

Mayflower Tours www.mayflowertours.com. 1225 Warren Avenue, P.O. Box 490, Downers Grove, IL 60515. 800-323-7604. Mayflower Tours offers special programs for senior citizens but does not have an age limit. Some senior travelers bring their grandchildren along on the tours. The minimum age for a child traveling on a Mayflower Tour is six years old.

Adventure Travel

If you have a spirited sense of adventure and lots of energy, consider traveling with one of these groups that specialize in challenging, exciting travel experiences.

GORPTravel (formerly American Wilderness Experience) http://gorptravel.away.com. 6707 Winchester Circle, Suite 101, Boulder, CO 80301. 877-440-GORP. E-mail: info@gorptravel.com. GORPTravel offers mature adults discounts on backcountry travel. Trips include a Bridger-Teton backcountry horseback trip in Wyoming, Sangre de Cristo Mountains horseback trip in Colorado, Mountain Sports Week Adventure in Colorado, a Colorado Surf and Turf Combo in Colorado, and an Alaska Wildlands Senior Safari Tour. In order to be eligible for the senior discounts you must be 65.

Outward Bound USA www.outwardbound.org. 800-88BOUND. Locations include North Carolina and Colorado. The Outward Bound organization is well known for its wilderness-survival courses that are aimed to help youngsters and young adults. Mature adults can also discover new ways to go beyond their limitations through Outward Bound's shorter courses designed specifically for older adults. Some of the courses have a special goal of easing the transition from career to retirement.

Be prepared to live in a tent, sleep in sleeping bags, and cook your own food. Good health is a requirement to participate. Adventures include: courses canoeing in the Florida Everglades, canoeing in the lake country of Minnesota, sailing in the Florida Keys, river rafting, desert backpacking or rock climbing on the West Coast, or white-river rafting or hiking in North Carolina.

Hostelling International USA (registered as American Youth Hostels) www.hiusa.org. 8401 Colesville Road, Suite 600, Silver Spring, Maryland 20910. 301-495-1240. E-mail: hostels@hiusa.org. This group coordinates more than 5,000 hostels in over 70 countries. The most relaxed and adventurous of mature singles stay in youth hostels both here and abroad, now that the international youth-hostel organization has removed all maximum age restrictions on the right to use their facilities. Particularly in the fall and winter months, when young people are in school, the predominant clientele of many youth hostels is today middle-aged and elderly! But even when sharing these multi-bedded rooms or dorms with young people, there is only an inexpensive charge, without a supplement. And you get to stay in a lively setting of international conversations and encounters.

Membership is $28 a year, but if you are 55 or older, you only pay $18. HI-USA offers low-cost adventure trips and educational and cultural tours at several destinations. You can tour all over the world by van, minibus, train, or bicycle. Some of their trips include: traveling by van to European cities; cycling in New England in the fall; a trip to the mountains, glaciers, and lakes of Alaska; five weeks by train and ferry through Europe; and hiking in the San Francisco Bay area.

Adventure Women www.adventurewomen.com. 300 Running Horse Trail, Bozeman, MT 59715. 800-804-8686 or 406-587-3883 (outside United States). Exclusively for active women over 30, destinations include Timbuktu, the Amazon River, Alaska, the Sonoran Desert and Southern France.

Africa Guide www.africaguide.com. Detailed information on traveling in 51 countries in Africa.

Eldertreks www.eldertreks.com. 800-741-7956. World's first travel company dedicated exclusively to people over 50. The group explores the culture and nature of a destination while traveling sensitively in small groups of 16 people or less. All trips involve walking and some include hiking in rainforests, deserts or mountain environments.

Pedal Power: Bike Trails

If you are a serious biker, you may want to consider taking a trip along the 4,250 miles of the America trail. This trail begins in Astoria, Oregon and goes to Yorktown, Virginia, winding its way across the country through small American towns. Campgrounds and inexpensive bike inns are situated along the way.

There are also several excellent companies that do nothing but plan biking tours, walking/hiking tours and other types of adventure travel. These companies offer trips all over the world for all levels of biking enthusiasts. Trips range from combination hiking/biking/backpacking vacations in Hawaii to luxury trips with gourmet meals and accommodations in four-star French chateaux and English castles. Check with your travel agent for information and brochures. Or check the listings in the back of some of the dozens of very interesting and informative travel magazines available at your local bookstore or magazine stand. Many of these companies advertise in the directories of these magazines.

U.S. National Park System and Recreational Areas

Our national park system includes some of the most breathtaking, magnificent areas on this planet. These areas are maintained and preserved by the government for use by all people who wish to experience the depth of our precious natural resources and the richness of our cultural history. Travelers can enjoy educational, stimulating vacations visiting our national parks, national wildlife reserves, recreation areas, monuments, and historic sites.

Some of these sites include: craters, swamps, seashores, caves, trading posts, battlefields, ships, military parks, historic homes, sand dunes, waterfalls, cliff dwellings, volcanoes, and giant redwood forests.

Information on national parks, historic sites, and monuments in the areas you plan to visit can be obtained online at the National Park Service web site: www.nps.gov.

Since observing wildlife is a recreational hobby shared by many mature adults, you may want to visit one of the 450 National Wildlife Refuges that comprise over 90 million acres of lands and waters. Write to: Division of National Refuges, U.S. Fish and Wildlife Service, Department of the Interior, Washington, DC 20240, for brochures and information. Or look up the web site: www.fws.gov.

There are 156 national forests stretching from Alaska to Puerto Rico that offer exciting opportunities for outdoor adventure. For a copy of "National Forest Vacations," write: U.S. Department of Agriculture, Forest Service, Information Center, 1400 Independence Avenue SW, Washington, DC 20250. Each regional office of the Forest Service has maps and literature about recreational facilities in the national forests. Visit their web site at www.fs.fed.us.

For information write to Regional Forester, USDA Forest Service at an area office listed below:

Alaska Region, 709 W. 9th St., Room 213A, Juneau, Alaska. 907-586-8806.

Pacific Southwest Region, 1323 Club Drive, Vallejo, California 94592. 707-562-8737.

Eastern Region, 626 East Wisconsin Avenue, Milwaukee, Wisconsin 53202.

Rocky Mountain Region, 740 Simms St., Golden, Colorado 80401. 303-275-5350.

Intermountain Region, Federal Building, 324 25th St., Ogden, Utah 84401. 801-625-5306.

Northern Region, Federal Building, 200 E. Broadway, P.O. Box 7669, Missoula, MT 59807. 406-329-3511.

Pacific Northwest Region, P.O. Box 3623, 333 SW First Avenue, Portland, Oregon 97208-3623. 503-808-2468.

Southwest Region, 333 Broadway SE, Albuquerque, New Mexico 87102. 505-842-3292.

Southern Region, 1720 Peachtree Road NW, Atlanta, Georgia 30309. 404-347-7478.

Some organizations offer wilderness trips in the national forests. Trips are organized with regard to differing levels of ability, with several designed with mature adults in mind. For information write:

The Wilderness Society www.wilderness.org. 1615 M Street, NW, Washington, DC 20036. 800-THE-WILD (800-843-9453).

New England Hiking Holidays www.nehikingholidays.com. P.O. Box 1648, North Conway, New Hampshire 03860. 800-869-0949.

The America the Beautiful Passes

National Parks and Federal Recreation Lands Annual Pass (formerly Golden Eagle Passport)

This is an entrance pass to those national parks, monuments, historic sites, recreation areas, and national wildlife refuges that charge an entrance fee. It also covers entrance fees at sites managed by the U.S. Fish and Wildlife Service, the U.S. Forest Service, and the Bureau of Land Management. The Annual Pass costs $80 and is valid for one year from any date of purchase. You may purchase an Annual Pass at any NPS entrance fee area, by calling 888-ASK-USGS ext. 1, or via the Internet at http://store.usgs.gov/pass. In 1999, President Clinton purchased a Golden Eagle Passport at Grand Tetons.

The Annual Pass does not cover or reduce use fees, such as fees for camping, swimming, parking, boat launching, cave tours, or concessions. It is valid for entrance fees only. The Annual Pass admits the pass holder and any accompanying passengers in a private vehicle if a park has a per vehicle entrance fee. Where a per-person entrance fee is charged, the Annual Pass admits the pass holder and three additional adults. (Children under 16 are always admitted free.)

National Parks and Federal Recreation Lands Senior Pass (formerly Golden Age Passport)

This is a lifetime entrance pass to national parks, monuments, historic sites, recreation areas, and national wildlife refuges for those 62 years or older. The Senior Pass has a one-time processing charge of $10. You must purchase a Senior Pass in person. It is not available by mail or telephone. This can be done at any NPS facility that charges an entrance fee. At time of purchase, you must show proof of age (62 years or older) and be a citizen or permanent resident of the United States.

The Senior Pass admits the pass holder and any accompanying passengers in a private vehicle. At per-person fee areas, the passport admits the pass holder and three additional adults (children under 16 are admitted free).

The Senior Pass also provides a 50% discount on federal use fees charged for facilities and services such as fees for camping, swimming, parking, boat launching, or cave tours. It does not cover or reduce special recreation permit fees or fees charged by concessionaires.

National Parks and Federal Recreation Lands Access Pass (formerly Golden Access Passport)

This is a free lifetime entrance pass to national parks, monuments, historic sites, recreation areas, and national wildlife refuges for persons who are blind or permanently disabled. It is available to citizens or permanent residents of the United States, regardless of age, who have been determined to be blind or permanently disabled. You may obtain an Access Pass at any entrance fee area by showing proof of medically determined disability and eligibility for receiving benefits under federal law.

The Access Pass also provides a 50% discount on federal use fees charged for facilities and services such as fees for camping, swimming, parking, boat launching, or cave tours. It does not cover or reduce special recreation permit fees or fees charged by concessionaires.

CHAPTER 4

Your Finances, Retirement and Insurance Made Easy

Finances and financial security, how to live within our means, and finding safe ways to invest our money are all major concerns for mature adults. In our "earning years," making money is our primary concern. As we approach retirement, keeping it becomes our main focus.

Retirement plans abound. There are seemingly endless numbers of investment firms, brokers, and counselors who would like to help you invest your money for retirement (which, of course, generates fees and commissions for them). Although there are many different types of plans available, I am going to show you how to get the best free and low-cost retirement savings investment advice, as well as how to find special savings available only to mature adults. I will also examine both how to obtain free health care

(when available) and how to find the most cost effective health care benefits and programs. As complex as
these issues seem, there are sources of information to
help us better understand them.

Free Stuff from the Bank

With banks and savings and loans in fierce competition for your funds, there has emerged a whole new
arena of privileges, perks, and special programs for
seniors. It is estimated that some 63 million Americans
age 50 and older hold approximately two thirds of all
bank savings deposits, and approximately 80 percent
of savings and loan deposits. It's not difficult to understand why banks and S&Ls are literally fighting for
these funds. In most cases the rate of investment return
is virtually the same among competing institutions, so
they have come up with all kinds of ways to entice
us into saving with their particular organization. This
translates into free benefits for seniors including:

- Free online banking
- No or low-fee ATM-only or express checking
  account
- Free checking accounts
- Free safe deposit boxes
- Free photocopying
- Added percentage points on invested funds
- Free checks
- Free notary service
- Free telephone and wire service transfers

- Free traveler's checks, cashier's checks and money orders
- Newsletters
- Waiver of service charges on bankcard membership
- Overdraft protection on checking accounts
- Seminars on tax-free investing, health, and fitness
- Free subscriptions to senior publications
- Travel discounts
- Membership in dining clubs
- Discounts on merchandise, entertainment, dental care, vitamins, eyewear, automobiles

These are some of the "extras" banks offer seniors and preferred customers to gain their business and lasting loyalty. Once you open an account or buy a CD, these banks are hoping you'll become interested in their trust services, home-equity loans, automobile loans, reverse mortgages, etc.

As in other industries, senior discounts and services are not always advertised or disclosed at first glance. You need to inquire as to what benefits you can receive. Make a list of the kinds of "extra" services you feel are important and present them to the bank officer responsible for new accounts. They may just offer you what you want. When deciding where to entrust your funds, compare requirements for maintaining minimum balances, service charges, and interest rates.

If you feel that your bank is not handling you or your business correctly you can turn to your State Banking Commissioner with your complaint. If you cannot resolve your problems with your bank (they are charging you too many fees, not approving loans, not offering basic services), then contact the Banking Commissioner's office and they will make an investigation. You can find the office in the government pages of your local phone directory.

If you are concerned about whether your deposited funds are insured (Treasury Bonds and certain notes are not), contact your nearest regional Federal Deposit Insurance Corporation office or the Division of Supervision and Consumer Protection, FDIC, 550 17th St., NW, Washington, DC 20429. 877-ASKFDIC (877-275-3342). You can also look up your local institution online at the web site: www.fdic.gov. They answer questions and take complaints regarding FDIC regulated institutions and your FDIC insured deposit. They also publish information on financial reports and the compliance of different institutions, free brochures and a quarterly newsletter.

Tax Relief

If you need information or help with your taxes, the IRS offers free publications on a large number of tax topics. In fact, there is an IRS publication that covers just about every item that appears on a Form 1040. Although these publications go into great detail, they are written simply and accurately. There is even a publication that contains a list of all the other free publications entitled: Guide to Free Tax Services. You can receive these publications by:

1. Calling the IRS's toll-free number 800-TAX-FORM (800-829-3676);

2. Going to your local IRS office, post office, bank, or library and seeing whether their supply of bulletins includes what you are looking for; or

3. Writing the Forms Distribution Center for your state (the address is listed in the Form 1040 booklet).

The IRS also has a toll-free volunteer telephone tax assistance number for specific questions on filling out your forms. This service, called Volunteers In Tax Assistance (VITA), works best for those with simple returns. The number is: 800-829-1040. For more complex tax returns, a professional tax preparer, tax service, or accountant is recommended.

Copies of all IRS forms and help on how to fill them out is available online at www.irs.gov.

Special Note: To read documents by the IRS, you will need a copy of Adobe Acrobat Reader on your computer. You can get a free copy of this software at www.adobe.com.

"Protecting Older Americans Against Over-payment of Income Taxes," is a free publication published by the Senate Special Committee on Aging. The purpose of this publication is to ensure that older Americans understand and claim all the legal deductions they are entitled to. Write for it at: Special Committee on Aging, U.S. Senate, G31 Dirksen Senate Office Building, Washington DC 20510. 202-224-5364. Or you can look them up at www.aging.senate.gov.

In addition, the AARP www.aarp.org/taxaide has over 8,000 Tax-Aide service sites manned by volunteer tax counselors who help low- and moderate-income taxpayers over 60 with filing their income tax returns. For information call your local AARP chapter or check their web site.

H&R Block www.hrblock.com has downloadable software that you can check to make sure everything is in the right place on your tax return.

CCH Internet Tax Research Network www.cch.com provides helpful hints about preparing for tax season and filing your individual return.

The search engine YAHOO! has a Tax Center www.yahoo.com/government/taxes that will help you find other tax help on the Internet. Their directory of links is comprehensive and should lead you to answers to your questions.

Retirement Recommendations

There are several sources of free and low cost information and advice on how to prepare for retirement. The National Institute on Aging www.nia.nih.gov

publishes numerous booklets covering retirement topics including:

NIA Publications Catalog, with information on the programs and resources of the National Institute on Aging;

"There's No Place Like Home—For Growing Old" a do-it-yourself planner for people without pre-retirement counseling services provided by their jobs;

"Good Nutrition, It's A Way of Life," which discusses senior nutrition;

"Crime and Older People," a wallet-size folder that outlines ways older folks can protect themselves against rip-offs, frauds, and swindlers.

The above and other information is available online at www.aoa.gov and www.hhs.gov.

Retirement Planning Associates www.retirement-planning.com. 818-781-7721. At what age can you afford to retire? RPA will help you decide.

Metlife offers a large variety of free brochures in a series that covers insurance, business, money, health and family issues. Call them at 800-638-5433 or check on their web site for the latest information: www. met life.com. The series is called "Life Advice." You can also write MetLife at 200 Park Avenue, New York, NY 10166.

Financial Engines on the Web www.financialeng ines.com. Sign up and receive a free prospectus/outlook.

The Metlife Mature Market Institute. Information geared for those 50 and older. Contact the Metlife Mature Market Institute at: 57 Greens Farms Road, Westport, CT 06880. 203-221-6580.

Wachovia Retirement Services (formerly American Express Retirement Services) www.wachovia.com/ myretireplan. Wachovia offers a free Retirement Kit. It contains two guides with valuable facts and information, and an easy-to-use savings calculator to help you understand:

- How much you will likely need to save each month for retirement;
- Options to consider for retirement plan distribution;
- Ways to invest your money now (it depends on your assets, and your tolerance for risk);
- How to help make sure your family is financially protected.

You can access the planner online.

Another source of information is Commerce Clearing House (CCH) www.cch.com. CCH publishes a variety of retirement planning booklets and reports. You can order them online at the web site, by calling the 800 number or writing them. Search for "retirement" at the web site to find the information you need. Commerce Clearing House, Inc. 4025 W. Peterson Ave., Chicago, IL 60646 or call them toll-free at 800-449-6439.

The Washington, D.C.-based National Reverse Mortgage Lenders Association is a national nonprofit trade association for financial services companies that originate, service, and invest in reverse mortgages. A reverse mortgage is a loan available to homeowners 62 and older. It allows them to address their retirement needs by converting part of the equity in their home into tax-free income, without having to sell their home, give up title or take on a new monthly mortgage payment. The association's web site www.reversemort gage.org has information about the specific reverse mortgage products available and the process of getting a reverse mortgage. It also includes a list of reverse mortgage lenders in each state, contact information and products they offer.

AARP explains the subject of reverse mortgages in detail in a free booklet, "Homemade Money: A Consumer's Guide to Reverse Mortgages." It's available for free online at www.aarp.org/revmort.

John Hancock Financial Services www.jhancock. com. John Hancock Mutual Funds, 1 John Hancock Way, Suite 1000, Boston, MA 02217. 800-225-5291. You can learn all about Mutual Funds and how to invest in them at the John Hancock web site. There are also IRA calculators at the site, so you can calculate what you'll need to invest to retire comfortably.

The Arthritis Foundation Planned Giving Committee www.arthritis.org organizes volunteer attorneys and financial planners who speak on such topics as estate, financial, and tax planning. These seminars and workshops are offered free to the general public. Contact your local chapter of the Arthritis Foundation for a copy of the calendar of programs in your area. They also offer financial planning information online at: www.arthritis. org/resources/Financial_Planning/Introduction/finan cial_intro.asp.

The AFL-CIO offers a wide variety of information on how to enjoy your retirement to the fullest at this web site: www.aflcio.org.

MassMutual (formerly New England Mutual Life Insurance Company) www.massmutual.com. Mass-Mutual offers full retirement information on their site, including a "Retirement Contribution Protection Calculator," and current performance of the leading mutual funds. 1295 State Street, Springfield, MA 01111-0001. 800-228-2479.

Your financial planner, accountant, insurance agent, or securities broker should be able to advise you on your choices of investment vehicles for safeguarding your money and insuring income for your and your family's future. Mutual funds, stock funds, bond funds, CDs, money market funds, tax-free income funds, taxable-income funds, growth-income funds, fixed-income funds, IRAs, Keoghs, annuities, reverse mortgages, living trusts, 401(k) plans, etc., are just some of the investment alternatives and opportunities available in today's complex financial marketplace.

If you want to make sure your financial advisor/planner, money manager, stockbroker or sales representative has not had any legal problems or disciplinary actions brought against them, you can call the toll-free hotline run by the Financial Industry Regulatory Authority. They have information on civil judgments, criminal judgments, indictments, arbitrations, disciplinary actions and other actions taken by securities regulators. Call them at 301-590-6500 or look them up online at www.finra.org.

You can also run a background check on investment brokers by calling the hotline of the North American Securities Administrators Association www.nasaa.org. 202-737-0900. They will tell you who to call in your state.

The Securities and Exchange Commission www.sec.gov will also do a full background check on any company that offers public stock or on any brokerage firm. In addition, they also publish several free publications on investing wisely and safely. Write them at the Securities and Exchange Commission, Office of Consumer Affairs, 100 F St., NE, Washington, DC 20549. Tel: 202-942-8088, 800-SEC-0330 (publications line).

If you are looking for a financial advisor or planner contact the Financial Planning Association (FPA) (formerly The International Association for Financial Planning) www.fpanet.org. 1600 K Street, NW, Suite 201, Washington, DC 20006. 800-322-4237. To receive the free booklet "Planning for the Stages of Retirement," send a self-addressed stamped, business-sized envelope to: FPA, 1600 K Street, NW, Suite 201, Washington, DC 20006. Or view it online at www. fpanet.org/public/tools/retirement.cfm.

You can also contact the National Association of Personal Financial Advisors (fee-only planners) www.napfa.org. 847-483-5400, 800-366-2732. They will send you a list of their members and questions you should ask any financial planner in an interview before becoming a client. A professional money manager must be registered with the SEC. The Freedom of Information & Privacy Act Office of the SEC, 202-551-8300, or your state securities commission can check their records for you.

Financial Tip: Always get an independent second opinion, or investigate yourself before investing.

For preparing taxes and other financial services, a professional accountant should be a certified public accountant (C.P.A.), licensed by the state. The state board of accountancy (the number is among the state government listings in the phone book) will let you know if any disciplinary or licensing actions have been brought forth.

A professional insurance agent should be a C.L.U., meaning chartered life underwriter or C.P.C.U., chartered property/casualty underwriter. Your state insurance commission (the number is in the state government listing section of your phone book) can give you records of disbarment.

For advice on buying, selling, or investing in real estate, work with a real estate broker or sales agent who is licensed by the state. They should also be a member of the National Association of Realtors or the local board of Realtors. Your state real estate commission (again, the number is in the state government listings in the phone book) can alert you to any past problems. Unless you know your agent well, investigate and get independent advice before buying.

Older Americans can get help coping with high heating bills and weatherizing their homes through state and federal programs. Call the Low-Income Home Energy Assistance Program at 866-674-6327 or go on-line at www.liheap.ncat.org. For state Weatherization Assistance Programs, visit www.eere.energy.gov/weatherization to find out who to call in your state.

An interesting and free source of information on investing for retirement can be found in the columns and features of senior magazines and newspapers. Most publications have a regular section on personal finance and/or money matters. A variety of questions pertaining to seniors are addressed in these pages. Their in-depth articles can help clarify and explain a lot of the confusion regarding money and investments. Local libraries and senior citizen centers subscribe to most of these publications. They are also distributed free in markets and some restaurants.

Where to Go for Answers on Medicare and Insurance

You will probably qualify for Medicare at age 65, but the program currently only covers little more than a third of actual medical costs. Chances are you will need either a medical supplement policy or an all-inclusive HMO or health insurance program to add to or replace Medicare. Medicare was never intended to be an all-inclusive health insurance program, and these supplemental policies offer coverage and benefits not covered by Medicare.

Trying to make sense of the several health coverage options that are available can be difficult and confusing; however, there are sources of information and education to help you understand these options.

The toll free Medicare Hotline, 800-MEDICARE, assists seniors in their questions and will refer them to local offices. They also publish and distribute free information booklets including: "Guide to Health Insurance for People with Medicare," "Medicare Coverage of Kidney Dialysis and Kidney Transplant Services," "Medicare: Hospice Benefits," and "Medicare and Other Health Benefits." Many of these publications are also available in Spanish. You can also write them at:

Centers for Medicare and Medicaid Services, 7500 Security Blvd., Baltimore, MD 21244 or check the information on their web site: www.medicare.gov.

"Medicare and Home Health Care," and "Staying Healthy at 50+,"are available through the Consumer Information Catalog www.pueblo.gsa.gov, Federal Citizen Information Center, Dept. WWW, Pueblo, CO 81009. 888-878-3256.

The Health Insurance Association of America www. hiaa.org, 601 Pennsylvania Ave., NW, Suite 500, Washington DC 20004, 202-778-3200, has an excellent free pamphlet entitled: "Guide to Health Insurance," which includes information on Medicare supplement insurance. This document is also downloadable from the web site.

The Health Insurance Counseling and Advocacy Program (HICAP) www.aging.ca.gov/html/programs/hicap.html of the California Dept. of Aging and the Legal Services Trust Fund organizes free educational programs and seminars on Medicare and HMOs through its Medicare Advocacy Project (MAP). MAP is an independent, nonprofit organization not affiliated with Medicare or any insurance company or Health Maintenance Organization. Senior citizen clubs, community centers, hospitals, medical centers and related organizations can schedule one of their specialists for a presentation. Some of the topics covered include: "Nuts and Bolts of Medicare," "Who Pays for Skilled Nursing and Long-Term Care?," "Filling the Medicare

Gaps," "What Supplemental Insurance Can Do," and "What You Should Know Before Joining an HMO." For information on their programs call 800-434-0222.

The Arthritis Foundation will send you a free booklet on choosing a health plan to cover all your needs. Write them at P.O. Box 7669, Atlanta, GA 30357.

The Social Security Administration provides a free booklet on survivors' benefits. It's available online at www.ssa.gov/pubs/10084.html. Or you can order it by calling 800-772-1213 and asking for publication 05-10084.

The Life & Health Insurance Foundation for Education, a non-profit group, offers a variety of information online to help you through the maze of terms, plans, and how much you should pay. This includes a glossary of common terms, information on the types and sources of insurance, and the costs you should pay. Call them at 202-464-5000 or visit their web site: www.life-line.org.

The Government Accountability Office (GAO) www.gao.gov wants to make sure you understand all the ramifications of long-term care insurance and the problems that can result from not paying premiums through your later years. Their series of free reports are available online or can be requested by writing: U.S. Government Accountability Office, 441 G Street, NW, Washington, DC 20548.

Aetna U.S. Healthcare Golden Medicare Plan www.
aetna.com/members/group/medicare/golden.html.
800-307-4830. Provides you with more benefits than
you probably get with Original Medicare alone or with
a supplement.

Most hospitals and medical centers also sponsor
their own free seminars on investment management
needs, health care, and life insurance. These are usually
coordinated through their senior or geriatric health
departments and are advertised in local newspapers,
senior publications, and mailings. Check with the hospitals in your area for a schedule of upcoming seminars.

In addition, some of the large federally qualified
health plan organizations sponsor lectures and presentations throughout the year at various locations.
Their schedules are usually advertised in local senior
publications and magazines. One example is Secure
Horizons www.securehorizons.com.

Senior newspapers and magazines, along with their
recommendations on investment and money matters,
offer a wealth of interesting and informative advice in
all areas of health care and insurance. Nearly every
publication has a regular feature or column answering
readers' questions on these subjects. These "health"
columnists and editors are specialists in their field
and offer consumers sound advice and referrals for
additional information. These publications also feature
monthly calendar listings of dozens of free lectures,
screenings, health fairs and expos, flu shot clinics,

etc. By taking advantage of these free community services, you can save yourself a lot of money on what is generally routine, preventive health care that costs a lot more with a private practitioner.

Automobile Insurance

Some insurance companies offer discounts on automobile insurance rates for seniors, who incidentally have better driving records than other age groups. Most independent agents represent at least one company offering special senior rates. Examples of insurance companies that give "senior rates" for good drivers include: State Farm Insurance Company, Nationwide Insurance, Liberty Mutual Insurance Group, and Allstate Insurance Company. The AARP also has an automobile insurance program, and several of the national senior organizations offer insurance discounts with membership. Your automobile club may also offer special discounts to their senior members who drive. Check with the individual organizations for their benefits.

CHAPTER 5

You're Never Too Old to Learn

Education is a lifetime process. Now, for the first time in many of our lives, we can choose to learn about the things we really want to know. Our choices cover a wide spectrum, from regular graded classes and curriculum to special classes offered specifically for mature adults. As seniors, we make the decisions on where to study, what to study, and how much or how hard to study. Now is the time to expand your horizons and learn for your own personal enjoyment and growth.

Practically every institution in the United States and Canada welcomes older adults into its regular programs, with a large majority offering reduced tuition and fees. If you wish to take courses for credit towards earning a degree or diploma, you may do so. However, if you simply wish to add to your knowledge, most schools will allow you to audit or monitor their classes.

In addition to the education you are receiving, going back to school is a wonderful opportunity to increase your social contacts and make friends. Younger students will benefit from working alongside a mature adult by gaining special insights from their life experiences and knowledge of the "real" world.

Learning Centers

A recent development in adult education that has gained popularity is the formation of adult learning centers offering a wide variety of short-term, practical, high-quality courses at reasonable fees. Most courses cost between $50 and $100 (except computer courses, which are usually under $200). Classes are taught by consultants, entrepreneurs, business owners, professionals, medical professionals, etc., who enjoy teaching adults in the community.

Programs center around topics such as finding new and unusual careers, improving relationships, self-improvement, real estate, hands-on computer literacy, money management, creative and career writing, hobbies, sports and recreation, living more spiritually, living healthier, entertaining, cooking, and other "nontraditional" topics. Classes generally meet once a week in the evenings. There are no grades, no exams, and no degrees. These programs are strictly for those who want to expand their knowledge in interesting, practical, and fun areas.

Below are names and phone numbers of adult learning centers around the country offering similar programs:

Boston Center for Adult Education www.bcae.org. Boston, MA 617-267-4430.

Discovery Center www.discoverycenter.cc. Chicago, Illinois. 773-348-8120.

Discovery Center www.oneonta.edu/academics/ scdisc. Oneonta, New York. 607-436-2011.

First Class www.takeaclass.org. Washington, DC. 202-797-5102.

Mt. Airy Learning Tree www.mtairylearningtree.org. Philadelphia, Pennsylvania. 215-843-6333.

The Learning Annex www.learningannex.com is a national franchise with centers located in Los Angeles, San Diego, San Francisco, New York, and Toronto. Since it first began 25 years ago, 1.3 million students have attended more than 132,000 learning Annex classes. For information on Learning Annex courses contact: The Learning Annex, Corporate Office, 48 West 37th St., 7th Floor, New York, NY 10018 or call the Learning Annex in one of the above cities.
New York Office: 212-371-0280
Los Angeles: 310-478-6677
San Francisco: 415-788-5500
San Diego: 619-544-9700
Minneapolis: 800-872-6639
Toronto: 416-964-0011

Auditing Seniors
Of all the travel privileges enjoyed by mature and senior citizens, one in particular is virtually unknown

and largely unutilized, and yet it is the single most valuable of them all: The right to "audit" courses free of charge (or for a nominal sum) at dozens of state and city universities. Though housing is generally available only in the summer, the free course privileges are offered throughout the year to seniors 60, 62 or 65 years of age and older (depending on the university), who then make their own housing arrangements for the non-summer months in motels or bed and breakfasts nearby.

Schools Admitting Seniors from Any State:

Boston University: The university's "Evergreen Program" permits senior citizens (58 and older) from anywhere to audit courses for $75 a course throughout the year. Currently, the university receives 200 to 300 senior auditors per semester, and does make some university housing available to them in summer. Write: The Evergreen Program, Boston University, 808 Commonwealth Avenue, Boston, MA 02215. Call 617-353-9852, or visit the web site: www.bu.edu/lifelong/evergreen.

University of Connecticut: Seniors 62 and older can audit as many classes as they choose for a fee of $15 per semester, space available. No requirement of state residence, and housing is available in summer on a space available basis in the dorms, and a 15-meal a week plan can be purchased. Phone 860-486-4631 for an application form to attend classes at the campuses either in West Hartford or Storrs, Connecticut.

University of Illinois www.continuinged.uiuc.edu/ oce-sites/conferences/poa.cfm. Persons 65 and older, from anywhere, can audit as many courses as they like (as long as they have the instructor's approval), other than labs or physical education classes, for a token fee of $15 per course (which, in summer, run for either four or eight weeks). But auditors have no university privileges (housing, meal plans), and must fend for themselves in that regard. Write: Office of Continuing Education, 302 E. John Street, Suite 202, Champaign, IL 61820. 217-333-2880; 877-455-2687.

Eastern Kentucky University: Senior citizens from any state, 65 and older, may audit any course for free, under the terms of the O'Donnell Scholarship, and enjoy university housing and meal plans, along with library privileges. Write: Admissions Office, 203 Jones Building, Richmond KY 40475.

University of Mississippi www.outreach.olemiss. edu/LifetimeLearner. Senior citizens from any state, 65 and older, can enroll for up to four credit hours per semester absolutely free, and can apply for university residence halls and meal plans on a space-available basis. One such applicant, in his late 70s, who feared his hearing wasn't up to par, was advised to tape lectures and later re-play what he failed to catch. The approach worked fine. Write: Office of Admissions, 145 Martin-dale, University of Mississippi, University, MS 38677 or call 662-915-7226.

University of North Carolina: Senior citizens 65 years or older are entitled to a tuition waiver for up to two courses per semester in distance learning classes. Non-matriculated students of any age, and from any state, can audit courses for $20 per course, if they have instructors' permission. Summer courses are presented in two, five-week sessions; but no assistance is given for housing or meals. Write: The Friday Center for Continuing Education, UNC-Chapel Hill, CB #1020, 100 Friday Center Drive, Chapel Hill, NC 27599. Call the main operator at 919-962-2211, to get the number of the professor whose class you wish to take.

University of North Dakota: Seniors age 65 and older can audit classes for free (except art & science classes that may have a lab or materials fee). Although housing and meal plans aren't available to auditors, meals can be purchased by anyone at university dining halls. Write: Enrollment Services, Box 8135, University Station, Grand Forks, ND 58202. 701-777-4463.

University of Oklahoma: Seniors 65 and older may audit courses free of charge, but have no access to university housing or meal plans. They must register within the first ten weeks of the semester, and then, only with the permission of the instructor. Write: Enrollment Services, 230 Buchanan Hall, University of Oklahoma, 1000 Asp Avenue, Norman, OK 73019.

Schools Admitting State Residents Only:
University of Alaska: State residents at the age of full Social Security retirement benefits can take (for

credit) or audit any course free of charge. They also receive library privileges, and—if enrolled for as many as 12 credit hours—housing privileges (costs vary in different residence halls) and meal plans (three meals daily for an entire semester, $1085). "Our student body is very impressed by persons in their mature age who wish to continue their education," says admissions officer Pamela Guzzy. Write: Enrollment Services, University of Alaska Anchorage, P.O. Box 141629, Anchorage, AK 99514-1629. 907-786-1480.

University of Arkansas http://ualr.edu/adults/index. php/home/senior-citizens/: State residents 60 and older can either audit or take courses for credit, free of charge, and are eligible for university housing and meals if they take a full-course load. Single rooms with all three meals daily are $2625 per semester; singles without meals are $27 a day in summer—a good time to attend short courses. You can request an advisor assigned by the Returning Students Association. For more information write: Adult Student Advocate, Office of Campus Life, University of Arkansas at Little Rock, 2801 S. University, DSC 216, Little Rock, AR 72204. 501-569-3370.

University of Colorado (at Boulder): At the Boulder campus only, state residents aged 55 and older can audit classes very inexpensively, but aren't eligible for campus housing or meal plans. Dues-paying members of the alumni association, which organizes these programs for the university, pay only $5 per class; non-members pay $60. The registrar with whom I spoke recalls overhearing an effort by an 18-year-old freshman to persuade a 70-year-old auditor not to drop a class they were attending together. Phone 303-492-8484, or write to The Senior Auditing Program, Koenig Alumni Center, Box 457, Boulder, CO 80309.

University of Delaware www.continuingstudies. udel.edu: State residents, 60 and older, can take as many classes as they choose, for free. Non-residents joining the "Academy of Lifelong Learning" for an $360 a year charge, can audit one course, attend a separate lecture series, and participate in various social activities. Housing ($593 for five weeks) and meal plans ($654 for five weeks and three meals daily) are available only during a summer session of five and seven weeks' duration.

University of Georgia www.georgiacenter.uga. edu: Except at the law and medical schools, state residents 62 years of age and older can take up to three five-hour classes per semester (either for credit or as auditors) for free. They can also secure university housing for only $1,874 to $2,363 per quarter if they enroll in twelve or more hours of courses per week. 1197 South Lumpkin St., Georgia Center for Continuing Education, The University of Georgia, Athens, GA 30602-3603. 706-542-2654.

University of Hawaii: In the normal school year only (fall through spring), residents of the state 60 and older can visit classes, with instructors' permission, free of charge. They receive library privileges, as well, but aren't eligible for housing or meal plans. They aren't allowed to visit in summer. Write: Office of Student Equity, Excellence, and Diversity, University of Hawaii at Manoa, 2600 Campus Road, SSC Room 413, Honolulu, HI 96822 or call 808-956-4642.

Idaho State University: Residents of Idaho, 60 and older, may audit by paying a flat fee of $20, plus $5 per credit–the average course consisting of three credits (i.e., three hours of instruction per week for one semester). Seniors are also eligible for university housing and meals: $2,775 for a single room throughout the entire year, all meals included. Write: ISU Admissions Office, Campus Box 8270, Pocatello, ID 83209.

University of Kansas: Persons 60 and over can audit as many courses as they wish, for free; but auditors aren't entitled to housing or meal plans. Call Office of Admissions: 785-864-3911 or write: KU Visitor Center, 1502 Iowa, Lawrence, KS 66045-7576.

University of Maryland: Under the "Golden I.D." program, seniors 60 and up can audit up to three courses at a time for about $178.50. While auditors aren't eligible for housing or meal plans, they do have library privileges. Write: Undergraduate Admissions, University of Maryland, 1101 Mitchell Building, College Park, MD 20742.

University of Massachusetts: By state law, seniors 60 and over, from any state, can take up to six credits per semester (or summer sessions) free of charge. Write:

Admissions Office, University of Massachusetts, Amherst, MA 01003. 413-545-0801.

University of Michigan http://casl.umd.umich.edu/ret_personspg/: At the Dearborn campus only, the "Retired Persons Scholarship Program" permits residents of the state 60 and over, who must be retired, to audit or take up to 3 courses for a flat fee of $150. Over 300 such seniors are currently enrolled, most of them studying art, history and philosophy. At the school's Ann Arbor campus, seniors 65 and over receive a 50 percent discount off normal tuition fees. Write: Retired Persons Scholarship Program, University of Michigan, 1100 SSB, 4901 Evergreen Road, Dearborn, MI 48128 or call 313-593-1183.

University of Minnesota: State residents only, 62 or older, can audit classes for free at all state campuses throughout the year; they join each class on a space available basis after the first day of instruction. University housing? It's sometimes available, mainly in summer. Write: Admissions Office, University of Minnesota, 240 Williamson Hall, 231 Pillsbury Drive S.E., Minneapolis, MN 55455 or call 612-625-2008 or 800-752-1000.

University of Montana: State residents 65 and older enroll for free by using the Senior Citizen Tuition Waver. Single rooms cost only $1,177 per quarter; all three meals daily costs $1,222 per quarter. Write: Student Affairs—Financial Aid Office, University of

Montana, Lommasson Center 218, Missoula, MT 59812 or call 406-243-5373.

University of Nevada: Fall and spring semesters only, 62 and older, can audit courses free of charge; during summer sessions, oddly enough, they pay 50 percent (about $78 per credit) of the normal tuition charge. University housing ($2,900 a semester, no meals) is available to senior citizens pursuing a minimum of twelve credits. Write: University of Nevada, Reno, Office of Admissions & Records, Student Services Building 2nd Floor, Reno, NV 89557 or call 775-784-4700.

University of New Hampshire: Residents of the state, 65 and older, can take up to two courses at a time for free, by paying a single $20 registration fee. Library privileges, yes; housing or meal plans, no. Write: University of New Hampshire, Department of the Registrar, 11 Garrison Avenue, Stoke Hall, Durham, NH 03824 or call 603-862-1500.

University of New Mexico www.unm.edu/~bursar/special.html. Seniors 65 and older can take classes (auditing or for credit) for $5 per credit hour. While they have library privileges, they have no on-campus housing or meal plans. Write: Office of Admissions, P.O. Box 4895, Albuquerque, NM 87196. 505-277-2446.

State University of New York: At every one of its many campuses, state residents 55 and older can audit classes (other than language or lab courses) free of charge, but only during the standard school year, and not in summer. Library privileges are also granted, but not housing or meal plans. Write to the branch you desire to attend, for instance, Office of General Studies, State U. at Albany, 1400 Washington Avenue, Room LI85, Albany, NY 12222. 578-442-5140.

Ohio State University www.continuinged.ohio-state. edu/CED_Pro60.html. By command of the legislature, anyone 60 or older from Ohio can audit classes free of charge ("Program 60"), and there is no restriction on participation in class discussion. Participants take classes on a space-available basis and do not earn credit. Currently, up to 200 seniors do so at any one time, by traveling to Columbus, Ohio, for five-week courses in summer, ten-week courses ("quarters") all other times. They can stay for less than five or ten weeks by dropping out before that time. Write: Office of Continuing Education, Ohio State University, 152 Mount Hall, 1050 Carmack Road, Columbus, OH 43210. Call 614-292-8860.

University of Rhode Island: Senior fees and waivers are being updated. Call for latest information. State residents only, 60 and older, are entitled to a waiver of all tuition charges other than a $25 registration, $15 activities fee and a $4 per credit fee (that goes towards library and computer services), but receive no housing or meal plans. Write: Enrollment Services, University of Rhode Island, Green Hall, 335 Campus Avenue, Kingston, RI 02881. Call them at 401-874-9500.

University of South Carolina www.usca.edu/conted/ seniorcitizen.htm. State residents age 60 and up who are retired can attend classes free of charge, and rent a double room in university residences for the entire year, for $2700 per person, including all three meals a day. Write: Adult Student Services, 901 Sumter Street, Byrnes 605, Columbia, South Carolina 29201. 803-777-9446. Admissions phone number for fee waiver information: 803-641-3366.

University of Utah: Residents 62 and older can audit as many classes as they care to, for a flat $25 fee per quarter (business management classes, art classes and labs excepted). They can also use the library and computer center, and the gymnasium and all other recreational facilities by purchasing a UCard for $10. Housing assistance isn't provided. Write: Lifelong Development, University of Utah, 1185 Annex, Salt Lake City, UT 84112 or call 801-581-6461.

University of Tennessee: Auditing of courses is free to residents 55 and older. They receive library privileges, too, but no housing or meal plans. The program is called Seniors for Creative Learning. Write: UT Professional and Personal Development, 313 Conference Center Building, Knoxville, TN 37996-1526. 865-974-0150.

University of Vermont: Residents who are 65 or older, receive free tuition for as many classes as they choose, and are also eligible for on-campus housing ($2800 per semester) and meals ($1,299 per semester).

"Younger students love the benefit of having elderly people in the class," says the school's registrar. Write: Continuing Education, 322 South Prospect, University of Vermont, Burlington, VT 05401 or call 802-656-2085; 800-639-3210.

University of Virginia: State residents only, 60 and older who have taxable incomes of less than $15,000, can audit up to three courses for free during summer sessions and the school year. Single rooms are also made available to them for $110 a week. Write: School of Continuing and Professional Studies, 104 Midmont Lane, P.O. Box 400764, Charlottesville, VA 22904. 434-982-5324

University of Wyoming: Persons 65 and older can take classes (even for credit) entirely free, depending on availability. And on-campus single rooms are available to them in summer at $992 for 8 weeks if they take at least 6 credits. Write: Division of Admissions, University of Wyoming, Dept. 3435, 1000 E. University Ave., Laramie, WY 82071. 800-DIAL-WYO.

Travel and Learn

Mature adults are among the largest percentage of national and international travelers. They also enjoy learning while they travel. As a result there are several extensive college campus and learning programs available worldwide that are tailored as learning experiences for seniors:

The Earthwatch Institute www.earthwatch.org. E-mail info@earthwatch.org. 3 Clock Tower Place, Suite 100, Box 75, Maynard, MA 01754. 800-776-0188 or 978-461-0081. The Earthwatch Institute sends its volunteers on scientific research projects (tagging turtles, measuring acid rain, interviewing rural residents), making use of a catch-as-catch-can array of housing accommodations (local schools and community centers, tents, and private homes) in which people are lodged as conditions permit.

Elderhostel www.elderhostel.org. Each year over 270,000 people fill classrooms all over the United States and around the world through Elderhostel, a nonprofit organization with the philosophy that education can be fulfilling and fun. Elderhostel has one- and two-week programs at more than 2,000 colleges, universities, research stations, and other educational institutions around the globe. Each offers low-cost sessions for people 55 years and older.

Classes are a blend of lectures, cultural events, local exploration, and social activity. They cover such diverse subjects as local history and culture, archaeology, the sciences, arts, and literature. The Elderhostel catalog is produced seasonally and filled with fascinating, enticing programs. I discovered the catalog at my local library and spent several hours poring over its wonderful courses.

The organization has begun adding brand-new "service programs" that take mature idealists to perform Peace Corps-like activities in emerging nations, or to conduct academic research in the environmental area, or to build low-cost housing in communities of the United States. While none of the latter projects breaks new ground, they enable mature persons to perform these tasks in the company of people their age. Initial responses to the new offerings have been strong.

The cost of Elderhostel is intentionally held to modest levels, consistent with traditional hostelling philosophy. Accommodations are simple and the food wholesome and nutritious. With several programs under $600, plus transportation, Elderhostel remains a stunning value and an inspiring opportunity for every mature American. If the cost is still prohibitive for you or someone you know, check on the "Hostelship" scholarship program which pays all expenses for those who meet the requirements.

As it continues to grow, this fine organization offers hope that the mature population of America will become the single best-informed, and therefore most influential, segment of our society. For information or to book a course, write Elderhostel, 11 Avenue de Lafayette, Boston, MA 02111-1746 or call 877-426-8056.

Osher Lifelong Learning Institute (OLLI) www.osherfoundation.org. This organization offers classes for mature students throughout the U.S. Headquartered at the University of Southern Maine, OLLI offers "educational experiences" at colleges and universities in 48 states (plus District of Columbia). Programs combine lessons in history and culture with lectures, field trips, and social activities.

The cost of membership is a moderate annual fee. Membership dues cover tuition for as many classes as will admit you. OLLI also sponsors annual trips abroad. For information write: OLLI National Resource Center, University of Southern Maine, P.O. Box 9300, Portland, ME 04104-9300. 207-780-4128.

Senior Ventures www.sou.edu/siskiyoucenter/seniorventures. This program features classes, theater tickets, and museum admissions as listed. Ashland-based programs include all meals and lodging in a campus residence hall. Travel adventures include first-class accommodations and most meals. Programs begin on the afternoon of the first day listed, and end with breakfast on the last day listed. Although the fee does not include transportation to the program, it does cover transportation to events during the program. Southern Oregon University, 1250 Siskiyou Boulevard, Ashland, OR 97520. 800-257-0577.

Language Study Abroad www.languagestudy.com. Since 1987, Language Study Abroad has presented highly professional "total immersion" language study programs in Mexico, Spain, France and Italy. Their goal is to have students become conversationally fluent as soon as possible in the languages of the country. Each program offers classes in small groups at all levels throughout the year. All of the instructors are native-born and educated in their respective countries. Housing is arranged with carefully selected local families to expose the student to the people and the culture, and to offer unlimited conversational practice.

Seniors, especially, are an important part of their program, since they often are the ones who have the time and desire to learn another language at this time of their lives. In addition, all ages of students come from universities, high schools, government agencies and international corporations to participate in this highly qualified and recommended program. They also offer similar programs in Spanish in Seville, Spain, and in French in Vichy, France. For more information write them at: Language Study Abroad, 1717 E. Vista Chino, Suite 7–234, Palm Springs, CA 92262. 760-416-0314 or visit their comprehensive web site at: www.language study.com.

Go to the Head of the Class

North Carolina Center for Creative Retirement (NCCCR) www.unca.edu/ncccr. The purpose of the center is to help enrich the lives of retirement-age people and, in fact, benefit Americans of all generations through educational and cultural programs. Eight programs are offered for those over 50 looking for ways to build fulfilling lives for themselves and others. The programs include: Senior Leadership Seminars in history, culture, politics, economics, and social structure; the Retirement Wellness Center for training seniors to be wellness advocates in their community; The College for Seniors, where classes are free from the pressures of testing and grades; Retirement Issues Forum; The Research Institute; the Retirement Planning Program; and The Senior Academy for Intergenerational Learning, where retired experts work with undergraduates.

Contact: The North Carolina Center for Creative Retirement, Reuter Center, CPO 5000, The University of North Carolina at Asheville, 1 University Heights, Asheville, NC 28804-8516. 828-251-6140.

Close Up Foundation www.closeup.org. For those 50 and older the Life Long Learners programs provide up close, behind-the-scenes educational tours of Washington, DC, and other places. The purpose is to give individuals a first-hand look at how government functions in our capital city. Activities include walks on Capitol Hill, seminars with key Washington personalities, bus tours, workshops and briefings on current events and issues, and social activities. These one-week programs give seniors a great opportunity to enhance their knowledge about our country's political process. Contact: Close Up Foundation, Life Long Learners, 44 Canal Center Plaza, Alexandria, Virginia 22314-1592. 800-256-7387.

"Go-60" Program www.aa.psu.edu/adult/go60.htm. Pennsylvania State University provides tuition-free enrollment in selected day or evening courses to seniors over 60 who are retired or employed less than half-time and are current residents of Pennsylvania, former Penn State students, or former Penn State employees. Contact: Adult Center, C112 Smith Building, Penn State Altoona, 3000 Ivyside Park, Altoona, PA 16601-3760. 814-949-5046.

The Smithsonian Institution www.residentasso ciates.org. The Resident Associate Program (RAP), a privately supported membership arm of The Smithsonian Institution, presents a wide variety of enriching education opportunities including cultural activities and public outreach programs. Resident members receive advance notice of programs and significantly reduced admittance fees for performing arts programs, lectures, films, seminars, studio arts, and courses. Contact The Smithsonian Associates, P.O. Box 23293, Washington D.C. 20026. 202-633-3030.

Chautauqua Institution www.chautauqua-inst.org. This institution sponsors summer weekends and one-week programs for folks over 55 at an 856-acre site on the shore of Lake Chautauqua, New York. A wide variety of educational programs with discussions, workshops, lectures, films, evening entertainment, and recreational activities are offered at this relatively inexpensive adult summer camp. Fees cover tuition, room, meals, and activities. For information write: Program Center of Older Adults, P.O. Box 28, One Ames Avenue, Chautauqua, NY 14722. 800-836-ARTS or 716-357-6269.

The College at 60—New York City www.fordham. edu/general/Undergraduate/College_at_Sixty3649.html. The Lincoln Center campus of Fordham University offers credit college courses in liberal arts subjects taught by Fordham faculty members. Actually available to adults over 50, the program includes a lecture series and use of all campus facilities. Contact: The College at 60 Program, Fordham College of Liberal Studies, 113 W. 60th St., Room 301, New York, NY 10023. 212-636-6376.

Duquesne University offers senior citizens over 60 discounts for full- or part-time study for one degree. For information write: Duquesne University, Office of Admissions, 600 Forbes Avenue, Pittsburgh, PA 15282. 412-396-6222 or 800-456-0590.

SeniorNet www.seniornet.org is a nonprofit organization that provides adults 50 and over with an education on how computer technologies and the Internet can enhance their lives and enable them to share their knowledge and wisdom. This program originated at the University of San Francisco as a research project to study the use of computer communication networking by older adults. Members throughout the United States and Canada communicate with one another and gain access to information of interest to them.

SeniorNet currently sponsors over 240 Learning Centers around the country for training, networking, and sociability. They also offer computer classes designed especially for older adults. There are more than 34,000 SeniorNet members linked by a national on-line computer network. Membership includes a quarterly newsletter, discounts on hardware and software products, discounts on car rentals and bed and breakfasts, and a discounted registration to the annual SeniorNet conference. Members pay a one-time fee to set up a network account (monthly subscription fees and hourly rates are extra). Members learn and teach others to use computers and communications technologies to accomplish a variety of tasks. They learn to desktop publish anything from a newsletter to an autobiography, manage personal and financial records, communicate with others across the country and the world and serve their communities.

SeniorNet operates SeniorNet Online on America Online (keyword: SeniorNet) and their own web site www.seniornet.org, where all individuals 50 and older, whether they are or are not members of SeniorNet, are welcome to participate in the hundreds of discussion topics offered on these sites. There are more than 600 message board discussions covering everything under the sun, including World War II memories, genealogy, technology issues, home and auto, politics and sports. For information contact: SeniorNet, 900 Lafayette Street, Suite 604, Santa Clara, California 95050. 408-615-0699.

Stress-Free Learning

There are several programs throughout the country affiliated with colleges, universities, and learning institutes that offer senior or adult oriented stress-free (no grades, no tests) classes. The courses are led by professionals who offer their expertise on a wide variety of subjects. Students pay an annual fee to the sponsoring university and may take as many courses as they wish (some also charge a reduced fee for individual courses). Included are campus privileges and use of campus facilities. Contact the individual campuses listed below for details on their programs:

Academy of Lifelong Learning www.academy.udel.edu. Academy of Lifelong Learning, 115 Arsht Hall, University of Delaware, Wilmington Campus,

2700 Pennsylvania Ave., Wilmington, DE 19806. 302-573-4447.

Center for Creative Retirement www.unca.edu/ ncccr. Reuter Center, CPO 5000, 1 University Heights, Asheville, NC 28804-8516. 828-251-6140.

Center for Learning in Retirement www.clirsf.org. 425 Market Street, 8th Floor, San Francisco, CA 94105. 415-543-3965.

Osher Lifelong Learning Institute at Duke www. learnmore.duke.edu/olli. E-mail: catherine.frank@ duke.du. Duke Continuing Education, Box 90704, Durham, North Carolina 27708.

Osher Lifelong Learning Institure at San Diego State University (formerly Retired Adults Program) www. ces.sdsu.edu/osher. SDSU College of Extended Studies, 5250 Campanile Dr., Suite 2503, San Diego, CA 92182. 619-594-2863.

Learning Center www.icmarc.org. E-mail: Investor Services@icmarc.org. Home of the Public Sector Retirement Specialists. 800-669-7400.

The Harvard Institute for Learning in Retirement www.hilr.harvard.edu. 51 Brattle St., Cambridge, MA 02138-3722. 617-495-4024.

Osher Lifelong Learning Institute at Northwestern University www.scs.northwestern.edu/OLLI. OLLI, 1840 Oak Avenue, Evanston, Illinois 60208.

Institute for Retired Professionals www.suce.syr.edu/community/irp/index.html. Syracuse University, 700 University Avenue, Syracuse, New York 13244-2530. 315-443-4846. New York location: 66 West 12th St., New York, New York 10011. 212-229-5682. www.newschool.edu. Miami Location www6.miami.edu/olli. University of Miami, P.O. Box 248276, Coral Gables, Florida 33124-2422. 305-284-6554.

The Lifelong Learning Institute http://undergrad.nova.edu/lli (formerly Nova College Institute for Learning in Retirement). University Park Plaza, 3424 South University Drive, Davie, FL 33328. 954-262-8471.

The Plato Society of UCLA www.uclaextension.org/plato. University of California at Los Angeles, 1083 Gayley Ave., Los Angeles, California 90024. 310-794-0231.

Personal Enrichment in Retirement www.hofstra.edu. 250 Hofstra University, Hempstead, NY 11549. 516-463-7200.

CHAPTER 6

Here's to Your Health

No one will argue that our bodies begin to go through changes after the age of 50. These changes are as normal and natural as anything else in our lives. At the same time, remaining strong, fit, and healthy will allow us to enjoy all the wonderful benefits of being a senior. Below are sources of information and preventive care to help you maintain the highest quality of health—your most precise commodity—throughout your life.

Since maintaining and improving health is such an important, universal concern, many dedicated individuals, groups, and nonprofit organizations offer free or low-cost testing, screening, and information on a variety of health concerns specifically related to the needs of older Americans.

Even with Medicare, Medicaid, and the numerous supplemental medical insurance plans, costs for preventive tests and exams are not always affordable. However, there are public and private facilities offer screenings, health assessments, and health education sessions as a public service. Look for advertisements for these screenings in the lifestyle section of your local newspaper. Some hospitals and medical facilities send out newsletters and mailings announcing times and dates of free medical testing for seniors. Check senior newspapers for calendar listings and ads on upcoming testing dates.

Many national associations, organizations, foundations, and manufacturers of medical equipment designate certain times of the year as "National _____ Prevention Month." For example, May is "Better Hearing and Speech Month," September is "National Breast Cancer Month," "Adult Immunization Week" comes at the end of October, and there is even an "Osteoporosis Prevention Week." During these designated weeks and months, vigorous campaigns and programs are implemented nationwide to create awareness of techniques of early testing and treatment for practically every illness from the flu to breast cancer.

Announcements of free and low-cost clinics associated with these yearly campaigns are usually made through local newspapers and publications.

Some companies use their medical departments or work with community agencies and local hospitals to provide a wide variety of screenings to determine employees' risk for developing certain diseases. Blood pressure screenings are the most common, but more comprehensive testing of blood and cholesterol levels are becoming available. Some companies will even provide follow up sessions with company doctors. This form of preventative care saves thousands of dollars in anticipated medical costs to companies offering medical insurance and coverage to employees.

There are also medical manufacturing companies that offer mobile testing services at local pharmacies, markets, shopping malls, health fairs, and health expos. Screenings include vision and hearing exams, pediatric exams, diabetic and glucose tolerance tests, mammograms, general dental screenings, body composition, pulmonary function tests, blood pressure, cholesterol, and stroke detection tests. Here is an example of a recent announcement in a newspaper "Check your blood pressure at the Beach Cities health District Health Fair on the Hermosa Beach Pier Plaza. The free fair offers 15 screenings, including tests for skin cancer and bone density, vision and hearing. You can also donate blood and learn about clinical trials and women's health." Be on the lookout for such announcements in your local newspaper.

Books and Information on Health

The National Institute on Aging (NIA) www.nia.nih.gov offers free publications covering many areas of health and aging. Some of their titles include: "Accidental Hypothermia," "Exercise Packet, Nutrition Packet," "Resource Directory for Older People," "The Menopause Time of Life," "What Is Your Aging IQ?," and "Women's Age Page Packet."

Of special interest to women are several women's health publications that describes the normal changes that take place during the aging process as well as conditions like arthritis and osteoporosis that become more prevalent in later years. The booklets provide a useful introduction to the challenges that mature women face and offer good tips on ways to deal with them.

The NIA also publishes a series called "Age Pages," which provide a quick, practical look at health topics that interest older people. There are over forty "Age Pages" covering the following areas:

Diseases and Disorders; Health Promotion; Medical Care; Medications; Nutrition; Safety; and Your Aging Body.

Write to The National Institute on Aging, Information Center, Building 31, Room 5C27, 31 Center Drive, Bethesda, MD 20892 for a complete list of their free publications or call 800-222-2225 or check for information online at www.nia.nih.gov/HealthInformation/Publications.

The Federal Citizen Information Center, Dept. WWW, Pueblo, CO 81009 publishes a quarterly "Consumer Information Catalog." This is a wonderful catalog that lists over 200 titles, covering a variety of practical, useful subjects such as drugs and health aids, medical problems, mental health, and general health. Examples of some current titles include:

"Dizziness"; "The Menopause Time of Life"; "Facing Surgery"; "Do-It-Yourself Medical Testing"; "The Colon"; "Food and Drug Interactions"; "Gallstones"; "Some Things You Should Know About Prescription Drugs"; "Heart Attacks"; "Osteoporosis." Call them at 888-878-3256. Web site: www.pueblo.gsa.gov.

The FDA Consumer is a publication by the U.S. Food and Drug Administration www.fda.gov. It provides information and reports on new medicines, their benefits and side effects, health advice of special concern to the elderly, and discussions of topics like sodium, osteoporosis, and generic drugs. The FDA Consumer is the official magazine of the FDA, which serves as the consumer protection agency responsible for food, drugs, medical devices, and other products used in daily life. Although the magazine stopped publishing in April 2007, many of the articles (available online) continue to be updated. Write: U.S. Food and Drug Administration, 5600 Fishers Lane, Rockville, MD 20857-0001. 888-INFO-FDA or 888-463-6332.

Write the American College of Surgeons, Office of Public Information, 633 North Saint Clair St., Chicago, Illinois 60611 for a free booklet on "When You Need an Operation." Web site: www.facs.org. E-mail: Postmaster@facs.org.

The National Heart, Lung and Blood Institute (NHLBI) www.nhlbi.nih.gov conducts research and answers questions on cholesterol, blood resources, obesity, asthma, high blood pressure, diet, and sleep disorders. They also distribute a variety of educational publications for consumers and professionals. Contact them for a free catalog of their publications: National Heart, Lung and Blood Institute Information Center, P.O. Box 30105, Bethesda, MD 20824-0105. 800-575-WELL (Heart Truth Line for Women) or 301-592-8573.

The American Heart Association <u>www.american</u> <u>heart.org</u> publishes free reports and brochures covering all types of heart disease. They offer a variety of positive/preventative tips for maintaining a healthy cardiovascular system. For a list of publications visit their web site or write: American Heart Association, National Center, 7272 Greenville Avenue, Dallas, TX 75231, or contact your local chapter of the American Heart Association. 800-AHA-USA1.

Diabetes is a challenging, but controllable disease. The more you know about this disease that affects millions of Americans, the more you can prepare and live a healthy lifestyle that will insure you enjoy life to the fullest. The National Diabetes Clearinghouse will furnish you with loads of information from early warning signs to diet and food preparation. You can get a complete list of their publications from their web site at <u>http://diabetes.niddk.nih.gov</u> or write them at: NIDDK Clearinghouses Publications Catalog, 5 Information Way, Bethesda, MD 20892-3568. 800-860-8747 or 301-654-3327.

Health Newsletters

Although there are several health newsletters available to the general public published by educational institutions, the John Hopkins Medical Letter, "Health After 50," is the first health newsletter specifically targeted for this age group. It is available from the Johns Hopkins Medical Letter: Health After 50, Subscription Department, P.O. Box 420179, Palm Coast, FL 32142.

386-445-4662. Check out their web site at: www.johns hopkinshealthalerts.com/health_after_50/index.html.

In addition, a growing number of companies and corporations are communicating health information to older workers and retirees through company news- letters and special mailings. Bank of America and Levi Strauss are two examples of companies that provide their retirees with free newsletters and self-help books containing information on health promotion and main- tenance. The Health Promotion Center, based at UC Irvine, has developed a series of materials out of their research that address the concerns of older adults. For information on these materials write: UCI Health Promotion Center, School of Social Ecology, University of California, Irvine. 949-824-5047.

More and more large community medical centers, teaching institutions and university medical centers are publishing informative and interesting community health newsletters. They include articles about testing programs, results of research studies, tips on maintaining health, articles on specific diseases or common condi- tions and dietary news and healthy lifestyle recipes. If you have a large hospital or community medical center nearby, give them a call and talk to their community relations department about getting on their mailing list.

National Organizations and Prevention Programs

Many national organizations provide free informa- tion on specific areas of health and disease prevention.

Since many of these conditions begin to appear when we are older, I've included groups that offer materials on the more common health problems of mature adults.

The American College of Rheumatology www.rheumatology.org offers information, brochures, and background publications on arthritis and other related conditions. Write: American College of Rheumatology, 1800 Century Place, Suite 250, Atlanta, Georgia 30345. 404-633-3777.

If you or a relative have arthritis and want more information, write to: The Arthritis Foundation, P.O. Box 7669, Atlanta, GA 30357-0669. The foundation has 70 chapters throughout the United States that offer courses and support resources designed to help arthritis patients and their families. 800-283-7800 or 404-872-7100. Web site: www.arthritis.org.

The National Jewish Medical and Research Center www.njc.org will send you free brochures and publications by writing: Public Relations, National Jewish Center, 1400 Jackson Street, Denver, CO 80206. Or call 1-800-222-LUNG.

Blue Shield of California www.blueshieldca.com. The Blue Shield of California web site includes valuable information on Senior Health and Wellness, from life events to mind and body, sexuality, and conditions and care. You can also read the latest health news here and sign up for a personal membership.

The National Osteoporosis Foundation, 1232 22nd Street NW, Washington DC 20037-1202, 202-223-2226, provides booklets and information regarding this disease, which is most prevalent in older women. In addition, the National Institute of Arthritis Osteoporosis National Resource Center has produced several Osteoporosis exercise booklets describing easy-to-do exercises designed to increase bone mass. Write to NIH Osteoporosis and Related Bone Diseases—National Resource Center, 2 AMS Circle, Bethesda, MD 20892, 202-223-0344. Web site: www.nof.org.

The U.S. Department of Health and Human Services www.hrsa.gov/hillburton administers a special funding program called the Hill-Burton Program, which requires hospitals and health facilities to provide services to people unable to pay. Those services are available to anyone residing in the facility's area. For information on the program, write your regional office of the Department of Health and Human Services or call the hotline toll free number: 800-638-0742.

The National Digestive Diseases Information Clearinghouse http://digestive.niddk.nih.gov/about. 2 Information Way, Bethesda, MD 20892-3570 offers free information on this subject. 800-891-5389.

Other national associations that provide free consumer health information include:

American Diabetes Association, National Service Center, 1701 North Beauregard Street, Alexandria, VA 22311. 800-342-2383. Web site: www.diabetes.org.

Alzheimer's Association, 225 N. Michigan Ave., Floor 17, Chicago, IL 60601. 800-272-3900. Although there is no cure or way to prevent the devastating effects of the progressive disease of Alzheimer's, there is an increasing amount of research being done on the subject in an attempt to find definitive causes and cures. The National Institute on Aging funds 28 Alzheimer's Disease Centers (ADC's) at major medical centers around the country. These institutions offer free diagnosis and treatment for volunteers for their research programs. If you know someone who might benefit from treatment, contact the medical college, university or medical institution in your area and inquire whether they provide services for Alzheimer's disease research volunteers.

Alzheimer's Disease Education and Referral Center (part of the National Institute on Aging) provides information on all aspects of Alzheimer's disease. They also have a database that includes references to patient and professional materials. Alzheimer's Disease Education and Referral Center, P.O. Box 8250, Silver Spring, MD 20907-8250. 800-438-4380.

The Alzheimer's Association www.alz.org provides information, referrals and support services to patients and families as well as training for caregivers. For a list of chapters around the nation, call the national help line 800-272-3900.

The Family Caregiver Alliance www.caregiver.org, which offers Alzheimer's training programs for families and health care workers, also has presentations on dementia and approaches to care. 180 Montgomery St., Suite 1100, San Francisco, CA 94104. 415-434-3388.

National Kidney Foundation, 30 East 33rd St., New York, NY 10016. 800-622-9010 or 212-889-2210. Web site: www.kidney.org.

Mental Health America (formerly National Mental Health Association) www.nmha.org. 2000 N. Beauregard Street, 6th Floor, Alexandria, VA 22311. 703-684-7722. Mental Health Resource Center: 800-969-NMHA.

In addition, some large university medical centers or community hospitals offer free membership programs, which include a variety of free services. For example, in Los Angeles, the UCLA Healthcare 50 Plus program helps people 50 and older maintain a healthy and independent lifestyle through a host of special benefits.

Additionally, the St. Johns Health Center in Santa Monica, CA has Senior TLC (Teaching Lifestyle Changes), a free membership program for adults 50 years and older, dedicated to helping seniors manage their health and wellness. Recent program activities included: Seniorobics, Tai Chi Chuan, Stroke Support

Group, Walking Group, Bingo, Blood Pressure Screenings, Senior TLC Self-Care clinic, Art Classes, All About Long Term Insurance, Women's Breast Conference, Tea and Travel, All About Retirement Planning, Healthy Cooking for the Holidays, and Senior TLC Annual Craft Fare.

These are extremely valuable and important services that are available completely free of charge. If you live in a metropolitan area or have a large university health center nearby, check to see if they offer any programs such as the one above.

Don't Lose Your Sight

For most of us our eyesight has already begun to change and may continue to change throughout our later years. In addition to changes in vision, more than 90 percent of Americans over 65 develop cataracts—but they vary in seriousness, and only a small percentage require surgery. Recent research has shown that drugs (including simple aspirin, and certain vitamins) may help prevent and significantly reduce a person's risk of developing cataracts. Some studies have even linked smoking and prolonged exposure to the sun to the risk of developing this condition. For free information send a self-addressed business-size envelope to the Customer Service, American Academy of Opthalmology, P.O. Box 7424, San Francisco, CA 94120-7424. 415-561-8500. Web site: www.aao.org.

Massachusetts Association for the Blind (formerly The Vision Foundation) www.mabcommunity.org. They are a non-profit agency serving children and adults with visual and other disabilities. For more information, call 617-738-5110. 200 Ivy Street, Brookline, MA 02446.

Prevent Blindness America (formerly The National Society to Prevent Blindness) www.preventblindness. org. 211 West Wacker Drive, Suite 1700, Chicago, IL 60606 has free fact sheets about eye care issues that concern older people. 800-331-2020.

The MD Foundation offers resources for information on macular degeneration. Write: P.O. Box 531313, Henderson, NV 89053. 888-633-3937. Web site: www. eyesight.org.

Pearle Vision Seniors Choice Program. There are over 850 Pearle Vision locations across the United States and Canada. Call 800-282-3931 to find out where your nearest Pearle Vision location is. They offer discounts through the AARP Health Care Options card. Your savings and services include:
- A complete and discounted basic eyeglass exam;
- A discount on comprehensive eye exams;
- Save up to 30 percent on eyeglass lenses;
- Save up to 20 percent on contact lenses.
Visit the web site at www.pearlevision.com.

More than 3 million Americans have glaucoma, yet half don't know it, since there are no warning signs. It's a leading cause of blindness for everyone over 60 and the No. 1 cause among blacks of all ages. January is National Glaucoma Awareness Month, and EyeCare America offers referrals for free exams to person who qualify, as well as free brochures to all. To learn more, call 800-391-3937 or visit their web site: www.eye careamerica.org.

The National Eye Institute (NEI) www.nei.nih.gov conducts research on prevention, treatment, diagnosis and disorders of the eye. They publish free booklets including: "Cataracts," "Don't Lose Sight of Glaucoma," "Don't Lose Sight of Cataracts," "Don't Lose Sight of Age-Related Macular Degeneration," "Don't Lose Sight of Diabetic Eye Disorders," "Diabetic Retinopathy." Write them at National Eye Institute, 2020 Vision Place, Bethesda, MD 20892-3655. 301-496-5248.

The Glaucoma Foundation has a very interesting and informative web site, www.glaucoma-foundation. org where you can learn the best ways to prevent blindness and receive good eye care. You can also write them for free information on eye care and prevention of glaucoma at: 80 Maiden Lane, Suite 1206, New York, NY 10038. Or call: 212-285-0080.

Keeping Your Skin Healthy

Another highly treatable problem that often does not show up until later in life is skin cancer. Since it sometimes takes 20 or more years to develop following overexposure to the sun, skin cancer's incidence increases with age.

May is "National Skin Cancer & Detection Month." The American Academy of Dermatology www.aad.org can tell you which doctors in your area are giving free screenings. Call them at 866-503-SKIN or look for announcements in senior newspapers. Or check directly with the health facilities, clinics, and hospitals in your area for when they conduct low-cost or free exams.

The Cancer Prevention and Control group can be reached by e-mail at: cdcinfo@cdc.gov. The toll free number is: 800-CDC-INFO.

The Elizabeth Center for Cancer Detection www.cancerdetection.org, a nonprofit corporation operating in Los Angeles since 1944, conducts periodic free skin cancer exams along with low-cost physical examinations for both men and women. 213-481-2511, Ex. 100 or 800-92-CANCER.

What You Should Know About Breast Cancer

The American Cancer Society www.cancer.org actively promotes nationwide low-cost mammogram programs during the year, especially in October during National Breast Cancer Awareness Month. Call: 800-ACS-2345.

Private and public health facilities cooperate with these screening and information programs:

Breastcancer.org www.breastcancer.org is a nonprofit organization that provides women with up-to-date information about breast cancer. They function as a resource network by offering on- and offline programs and chat rooms and featuring articles on every aspect of breast cancer, from diagnosis to recovery. They offer free informational booklets and brochures as well as tips on how to lower your risk of breast cancer. If you have any questions write them at: breastcancer.org, 111 Forrest Avenue, 1R, Narberth, PA 19072. 610-664-1990.

Finally, the National Cancer Institute publishes an informative booklet entitled, "What You Need to Know About Breast Cancer" (NIH Publication No. 05-1556). They also publish several booklets on other topics related to cancer including nutrition, detection, prevention, smoking, surviving cancer and more. Visit their web site at www.cancer.gov or call them toll free at 800-4-CANCER.

Pay Attention to Your Prostate

Many men past the age of 40 develop prostate disorders, which in most cases are treatable with a simple outpatient procedure. In Los Angeles, The Brotman Medical Center www.brotmanmedicalcenter.com offers free prostate screenings. Call the medical centers in your area to see if they offer similar screenings. The address for the Brotman Medical Center is: 3828 Delmas Terrace, Culver City, California 90232. 310-836-7000.

The National Kidney and Urologic Diseases Information Clearinghouse http://kidney.niddk.nih.gov

publishes a series of free publications on this subject. Titles include: "Age Page: Prostate Problems" and "Prostate Enlargement: Benign Prostatic Hyperplasia." These publications are available online or by writing them at: National Kidney and Urologic Diseases Information Clearinghouse, 3 Information Way, Bethesda, MD 20892-3580.

Don't Boo-Hoo the Flu

Another common concern among older adults is the flu. A yearly vaccine for seniors 55 and older is highly recommended, as well as a one-time dose of pneumonia vaccine. The idea that you can develop some kind of natural and lasting immunity to influenza is not true since flu viruses do change from year to year. The current vaccine has keen proven to be very safe and effective about 80 percent of the time, greatly decreasing the risks of complications from flu.

Free and low-cost flu shots are provided by dozens of county health departments, health maintenance organizations, nursing homes, and community centers. They are given at grocery stores, drug stores, local hospitals, senior centers, parks, banks, and other public sites.

The National Coalition for Adult Immunization (NCAI) www.nfid.org has a public education program that begins during Adult Immunization Week in October of each year. Booklets and information sheets are available through the NCAI, National Foundation for Infectious Diseases, 4733 Bethesda Ave., Suite 750, Bethesda, MD 20814. 301-656-0003.

Free flyers and brochures about adult immunization as well as immunization reports, presentations, and manuals are available from the Center for Disease Control Immunization www.cdc.gov/vaccines/pubs/default. htm. NIP Public Inquiries Mailstop E-05, 1600 Clifton Rd., NE Atlanta, GA 30333. 800-CDC-INFO (English) or 800-232-4636 (Spanish).

A free publication entitled, "Flu," is published by the National Institute of Allergy and Infectious Diseases, News and Publication Information Branch, 6610 Rockledge Dr. MSC 6612, Bethesda, MD 20892-6612. Check out the web site www.niaid.nih.gov for more information.

Taking Care of Your Teeth

Dental problems and tooth loss do not have to be serious issues for older people. In fact, losing teeth is not a normal part of aging. Over 60 percent of people 65 and older have their natural teeth. However, it is necessary to continue regular check-ups and treatment throughout your life. It has been proven that good oral health can affect and actually improve overall health. Unfortunately, Medicare does not pay for most dental care, and few older persons have separate dental insurance. This means the vast majority of dental services received are paid for out-of-pocket.

One way to reduce the high cost of dental care is through treatment at one of the 55 accredited dental schools in this country and Canada. Most of them provide patient care at 50 percent or more off most services. Many also provide special free services for the community-at-large, such as care to nursing home patients, oral cancer screenings at senior centers, and staff training to consumer groups. In addition, recent federal legislation has made the 15,000 nursing homes in this country receiving federal dollars directly responsible for the dental care needs of their residents. There are over 200 dental hygiene programs across the country that provide special services for older persons. Many state and local health departments support dental clinics that offer their services for free or on a payment basis. Services are usually restricted to those with limited income or special needs. To find out about a dental care or research programs in your area contact your local dental society (listed in the phone book) or write one of the following:

American Dental Education Association www. adea.org. 1400 K Street NW, Suite 1100, Washington, DC 20005. 202-289-7201 or 202-289-7385.

American Dental Association www.ada.org. 211 East Chicago Avenue, Chicago, IL 60611. 312-440-2500.

American Society for Geriatric Dentistry www.scd online.org/displaycommon.cfm?an=7. 401 North Michigan Avenue, Suite 2200, Chicago, IL 60611. 312-527-6764.

National Institute of Dental and Craniofacial Research www.nidcr.nih.gov. NIDCR Public Information & Liaison Branch, 45 Center Dr., Bethesda, MD 20892-2190. 301-496-4261.

For more information look up: www.ada.org/ada/prod/index.asp

Help for Hearing

The following include sources of free and low-cost hearing exams:

To find an otolaryngologist (ear, nose, and throat doctor), or otologist (ear-only specialist), write to: Physician's List, Association of Otolaryngology Administrators. 1844 Ardmore Blvd., Pittsburgh, PA 15221. 412-243-5156. Enclose an SASE to receive a free list of doctors in your area. E-mail: AOA@oto-online.org. Web site: www.oto-online.org

If you think you might have a hearing problem, you can contact the Hearing Loss Association of America (formerly Self Help For Hard of Hearing People) www.shhh.org. They offer low cost publications on dealing with hearing problems and a list of 200 support groups around the country. Send a SASE to: Hearing Loss Association of America, 7910 Woodmont Avenue, Suite 1200, Bethesda, MD 20814. E-mail: national@ shhh.org. 301-657-2248.

The Better Hearing Institute's Helpline gives information on all kinds of hearing problems. Contact American Speech-Language-Hearing Association, 10801 Rockville Pike, Rockville, MD 20852, or call 800-638-8255 for information on hearing and help in finding an audiologist (a professional trained to assess hearing loss). The toll-free number is 888-498-6699. Web site: www.asha.org.

Beltone Electronics www.beltone.com/pub/free Offer.asp, one of the largest manufacturers of hearing aids, offers free hearing tests at their centers during Better Hearing Month (May). They will also send a free non-operating model of their most popular canal hearing aid to show prospective users how tiny and light a hearing aid can be. Visit their web site to apply for a free sample at www.beltone.com.

The AARP www.aarp.org/money/wise_consumer/ smartshopping/a2002-10-03-WiseConsumerDifficult Hearing.html, publishes a report, "When Hearing Grows Difficult" (D13766), to help older people understand why hearing often declines with age and what products are on the market to help the problem. The report also offers tips on selecting the right equipment. To order a free AARP publication, send an e-mail to member@ aarp.org with your name, your full postal mailing address, and the title and stock number of the publication. If you do not know the title, but know the topic, describe what information you are looking for and they will try to match your request. Many of their publications are available online. Or write them at: AARP,

601 E. St. NW, Washington, DC 20049. 888-OUR-AARP or 888-687-2277.

Finally, there is a new online service called Free-HearingTest.com www.freehearingtest.com/test.shtml. This link will direct you to a webpage to take the test. When you reach the webpage, you receive complete instructions for taking the test, which consists of one continuous tone. You can also test your hearing with a variety of environmental sounds, including various forest animals, an airplane, and a lawnmower.

Hearing, Speech and Deafness Center (HSDC) www.hsdc.org. Seattle Office: 1625 19th Ave., Seattle, WA 98122-2798. 206-323-5770. Catalog Sales: 206-328-6872 or 1-888-328-2974. HSDC is a nationally unique, fully accredited independent agency offering a broad array of services tailored to help people with a variety of communication problems related to hearing loss and/or speech and language impairments. Approximately 20 percent of the region's population is hard-of-hearing, speech impaired or deaf. These people face challenges that affect them, their families, friends and colleagues.

HSDC rents assistive communication and signaling devices. Their target rental areas are (1) groups or conferences who need FM equipment, (2) hotel packages for guest rooms and front desks, and (3) personal alert pagers for post surgical patients who go home from the hospital and need a paging system for only a few weeks. If your business, social gathering or personal requirements dictate the need to rent assistive devices, call the store at 206-328-6872 or e-mail to store@hsdc.org.

You can learn about the causes of hearing loss, receive hearing aid information and the latest research on hearing related disorders from the National Institute on Deafness and Other Communication Disorders. Write them at: NIDCD, National Institutes of Health, 31 Center Drive, MSC 2320, Bethesda, MD 20892-2320 or call 800-241-1044; or visit them online at: www.nidcd.nih.gov. They will be happy to send you free brochures and answer your questions. The e-mail is: nidcdinfo@nidcd.nih.gov.

In addition to general problems associated with hearing loss, there are about 6 million people who suffer from tinnitus, a ringing in the ears of bell-like sounds. The symptoms of tinnitus, which occurs more frequently in older persons, cause many people to suffer from sleeplessness, stress, and job-related difficulties. These symptoms are sometimes referred to as Meniere's disease when they include vertigo and dizziness, and can also be associated with hearing loss and fluctuation. For information on tinnitus or a copy of a brochure titled "Information About Tinnitus" (include $1.00 plus $2.50 S/H) write to: American Tinnitus Association www.ata.org. P.O. Box 5, Portland, OR 97207-0005. 800-634-8978 (toll free within the U.S.); 503-248-9985. E-mail: tinnitus@ata.org.

Live for Tomorrow—Quit Smoking Today

Many older people dismiss it, but feet and leg pains may be warning signs of more serious disorders and shouldn't be dismissed. They could be symptoms of a circulatory disorder called peripheral arterial disease, or P.A.D. There are many causes of P.A.D.—all either preventable or controllable. They are diabetes, high blood pressure, high cholesterol and smoking. Smoking is number one. These can all cause restricted blood flow to the legs because of blockage in the arteries resulting in P.A.D. and possible further complications.

There are so many reasons to quit smoking that I won't list them except to say that you are guaranteed to live longer even if you've been smoking for years. According to the Centers for Disease Control's Office on Smoking and Health, it is worth it to give up smoking at any age. They have lots of information on the health risks associated with smoking and second-hand smoke.

Look up more information on their web site: www.cdc.gov/tobacco or write them at: Office on Smoking and Health, National Center for Chronic Disease Prevention and Health Promotion, Centers for Disease Control and Prevention, Publications Catalog, Mail Stop K-50, 4770 Buford Hwy., NE, Atlanta, GA 30341-3717. 800-CDC-4636. E-mail: tobaccoinfo@cdc.gov.

For helpful information on reducing your cholesterol and hypertension write: The Hypertension and Vascular Research Center www.wfubmc.edu/hypertension, Wake Forest University School of Medicine, Winston-Salem, North Carolina 27157-1032. 336-

716-5819 or The American Diabetes Association, Inc. www.diabetes.org, Attn: National Call Center, 1701 North Beauregard Street., Alexandria, VA 22311. 800-342-2383.

Relieving Your Aching Feet and Back

As for our feet and toes, studies show that nearly 90 percent of Americans suffer at one time or another from foot ailments. These can result in headaches, fatigue, grouchiness, and lowered productivity. Some of the more common foot ailments include bunions, heel spurs, corns and calluses, fungus infections, and foot cramps. Check with local podiatry clinics, medical centers, and private podiatry groups to get free or low-cost foot exams and an evaluation of what's ailing your feet.

Back pain affects millions of people and causes millions of dollars in lost wages and productivity from employee absenteeism because of the suffering it causes. Learn more about back care from the American Physical Therapy Association. Write them at: American Physical Therapy Association, 1111 North Fairfax Street, Alexandria, VA 22314-1488. 800-999-APTA or 703-684-APTA. They are also on the web at www.apta.org. Write for their booklet "Taking Care of Your Back."

The American Podiatric Medical Association website www.apma.org includes lots of free information on foot pain and arthritis, foot pain and diabetes and more.

Check out Spine-Health.com www.spine-health.com, a comprehensive web site on back pain and prevention.

Wear a "Real" Lifesaver

In recent years several companies have come out with medical alert tags and identification cards, which contain vital information for police, paramedics, and hospital staffs in case of a medical emergency. Although initially designed with children in mind, they have become very popular with older adults as well.

MedicAlert www.medicalert.org is a nonprofit organization whose sole purpose is to notify emergency health care professionals about a person's specific conditions. MedicAlert bracelets and necklaces alert attending persons to conditions such as asthma, heart problems, epilepsy, allergies or diabetes. A lifetime membership includes a steel necklace or bracelet engraved with your personal identification number and a 24-hour telephone number tied into a data bank in California. As a backup you also get an identification card. Personal medical information is updated each year. MedicAlert Foundation International, 2323 Colorado Ave., Turlock, CA 95382. To join, call 888-633-4298 or 209-668-3333 from outside the U.S.

Discounts on Drugs

Prescription drugs are one of the most hotly contested issues for seniors today. In many cases, it is nearly impossible to live on a reduced salary or retirement income and be able to afford medicines at today's prices. Even with the government programs and supplemental state programs, the cost of some daily medications is prohibitive. However, there are ways to help combat this ongoing problem and make drugs more affordable for mature adults.

To begin with, ask your doctor for as many samples as he/she will give you. Prescription drug companies are known to give away a lot of samples that doctors can pass on to their patients. This is especially useful when you only need to take the prescriptions for a limited or short length of time.

If you need to fill a prescription, ask your pharmacist for a generic version. This will contain the same ingredients as the name brand, but it many save you up to 50% or more.

Compare prices with drugs, just as you would anything else. Large chain pharmacy departments may offer a lower price than small independent merchants.

Ask your local pharmacy whether they offer senior discounts for medicines and prescription drugs, either through their own club or membership in a senior organization.

Don't overlook the fact that your health insurance or the coverage from you or your spouse's employer may cover a portion of prescription medicines.

Several senior citizen clubs and groups offer their members discounts on prescription medicines. Many of them offer mail-order services as well.

Albertson's, a nationwide chain of grocery stores, is aligned with SavOn Pharmacies operating over 100 stores throughout the U.S. Call 1-800-SHOPALB (746-7252) for specific store locations and discounts or visit their web site at www.albertsons.com.

CVS Pharmacies www.cvs.com with over 800 stores in 14 states covering the Northeast and California, also offer folks over 60 a 10 percent discount on prescriptions for in-store only purchases. They also offer a membership card called "Extra Care" which entitles members to special offers, discounts, and even college tuition savings plans. (Customers in New Jersey must be 62 or older.)

The American Association of Retired Persons (AARP) www.aarppharmacy.com will mail your prescription (as well as thousands of other drugstore products) at a discount and you don't even have to be a member. They have a special department for marketing products for diabetics. Orders are usually shipped within 24 to 48 hours. Call 866-202-4020 for a catalog.

Merck-Medco (formerly Merck-Medco Managed Care, LLC) www.medcohealth.com. Call your insurance company to see whether they have a contact with this drug company. You may qualify for discounts.

If you are lucky enough to live in one of the fourteen states that have special drug programs (State Pharmaceutical Assistance Programs www.elderweb.com/home/topics/State+Assistance) that give big savings for seniors who are not eligible for Medicaid and who don't have private insurance, all you need to do is qualify and you can begin saving immediately. The following programs will send you a form to fill out to qualify:

Arizona. Arizona Health Care Cost Containment System. Oversees programs and services of AHCCCS, Arizona's Medicaid managed care program. 801 E. Jefferson, Phoenix, AZ 85034. 602-417-4000. E-mail: MemberServices@azahcccs.gov. Web site: www.ahccs. state.az.us.

California. California Department of Health Services. Medical Care Services, MS 4000, P.O. Box 997413, Sacramento, CA 95899. 916-445-4171 or 866-298-8443. Web site: www.dhs.ca.gov.

Connecticut. Connecticut Department of Social Services. 25 Sigourney Street, Hartford, CT 06106-5033. E-mail: pgr.dss@ct.gov. 800-423-5026. Web site: www. ct.gov/dss/.

Delaware. Delaware Health and Social Services, Division of Medicaid and Medical Assistance, 1901 N. Du Pont Highway, Lewis Building, New Castle, DE 19720. 302-255-4454. E-mail: info@state.de.us. Web site: www.dhss.delaware.gov/dhss.

Also in Delaware, Nemours Health Clinic www.ne mours.org/service/pharmacy.html. 252 Chapman Road, Suite 200, Newark, DE 19702. 302-444-9100 or 866-390-3610.

Florida. Florida Department of Elder Affairs. Oversees aging programs in Florida, 4040 Esplanade Way, Tallahassee, FL 32399-7000. 850-414-2000. E-mail: information@elderaffairs.org. Web site: http://elder affairs.state.fl.us.

Illinois. Illinois Department on Aging, P.O. Box 19021, Springfield, IL 62794-9021; 800-624-2459 or fill out Form IL-1363, Circuit Breaker and Pharmaceutical Assistance Claim Form. Web site: www.cbrx.il.gov.

Indiana. HoosierRx, P.O. Box 6224, Indianapolis IN 46206-6224. 317-234-1381 or 866-267-4679. Web site: www.in.gov/fssa/elderly/hoosierrx.

Kansas. Kansas Department on Aging. New England Building, 503 S. Kansas Avenue, Topeka, KS 66603-3404. 785-296-4986. E-mail: wwwmail@aging.state.ks.us. Web site: www.agingkansas.org.

Maine. Maine Health and Human Services, Office of Elder Services, 11 State House Station, 442 Civic Center Drive, Augusta, ME 04333. 207-287-9200 or 800-262-2232. E-mail: BEAS.Webmaster@maine.gov. Web site: www.maine.gov/dhhs/beas.

Maryland. Maryland Pharmacy Program, P.O. Box 386, Baltimore, MD 21203-0386. 410-767-5800; 800-492-5231. Web site: www.dhmh.state.md.us/mma/mpap.

Massachusetts. Executive Office of Elder Affairs, One Ashburton Place, 5th floor, Boston, MA 02108.

800-243-4636 or 617-727-7750. Web site: www.mass. gov/?pageID=eldershomepage&L=1&L0=Home&sid =Eelders.

Minnesota. Minnesota Department of Human Services. P.O. Box 64838, St. Paul, MN 55164-0838. 651-431-2801 or 800-657-3672. Web site: www.dhs.state. mn.us.

Missouri. Missouri Rx Plan (formerly Missouri Senior Rx Program). P.O. Box 6500, 205 Jefferson Street, 14th Floor, Jefferson City, MO 65102-6500. 800-375-1406. E-mail: clinical.services@dss.mo.gov. Web site: www.morx.mo.gov/index.htm.

New Jersey. State of New Jersey Department of Health and Senior Services, P.O. Box 360, Trenton, NJ 08625-0360. 609-292-7837 or 800-367-6543 (inside New Jersey). Web site: www.state.nj.us/health/sen iorbenefits.

www.themedicineprogram.com. This site's function is to assist patients who may qualify to enroll in one or more of the many patient assistance programs now available. These programs provide prescription medicine free of charge to individuals in need, regardless of age if they meet the sponsor's criteria.

CHAPTER 7

Associations and Organizations That Work for Mature Adults

There are more people in this country over the age of 55 than there are children in elementary and high school. Mature adults represent a major influence and power that affects nearly every area of American life. In addition to their growing numbers, they control most of this nation's disposable income. As a consequence this group has become a prime target of today's marketplace and a major concern and focus for our lawmakers and politicians.

A large number of national, state, and local organizations, some independent and some linked by vast networks of affiliates, have been created over the past few decades in the United States and Canada. These groups act as advocates and protectors of the rights of those 50 and over. Together, they represent millions of voices demanding action, attention, and respect. Not only do they provide important information and powerful lobbying services, but many offer special discounts and services for seniors that allow them to enjoy and accomplish many things in life that they would otherwise be unable to afford.

Organizations and associations that operate specifically to serve the needs of mature adults are listed below. By learning about these different groups you can choose which ones most closely match your interests and concerns. There is an enormous amount of information as well as services waiting to be discovered. There are also endless avenues available for working with these groups to improve the quality of life for yourself and other determined, dedicated seniors.

Federal Agencies

Uncle Sam provides us with a wealth of information just for the asking. Below are government agencies that collect and distribute information to the public.

U.S. Department of Commerce
U.S. Census Bureau National Data Processing Center
Washington, DC 20233
812-218-3046

Within the Bureau of the Census is the Census History Staff. As an outgrowth of the collection of data from the census, the "Age Search Program" was begun. This program helps mature adults obtain personal historical information by requesting census records. These census records can help prove age and/or citizenship, and help to obtain a birth certificate, passport, or social security benefits.

National Library of Medicine (formerly National Center for Health Services, Research and Health)
Reference and Web Services
8600 Rockville Pike
Bethesda, MD 20894
888-346-3656 or 301-594-5983
www.nlm.nih.gov
This agency publishes reports on issues affecting the elderly, especially on the subject of long term care. Request their free publications.

Social Security Administration
Office of Public Inquiries
Windsor Park Building
6401 Security Blvd.
Baltimore, MD 21235
800-772-1213
www.ssa.gov
Local Social Security offices can help in finding out about senior programs, community groups, and activities in an area. The above toll-free Social Security Administration telephone number operates from 7 A.M. to 7 P.M. throughout the country. Call during off-peak hours, such as 7 to 9 A.M. and 5 to 7 P.M., to receive free information on Social Security Programs, card name changes, earnings statements, Medicare and Medicaid benefits.

Centers for Disease Control and Prevention
National Center for Health Statistics
3311 Toledo Road
Hyattsville, MD 20782-2003
800-232-4636
www.cdc.gov/nchs

This agency collects data regarding numerous health issues and produces reports for public use. Call them and request to be put on their mailing list. The free reports are published in pamphlets, which most often are summaries on issues of health. Any person on the mailing list is eligible for ordering the in-depth reports, usually 100 pages or more. Request the list of reports that focus particularly on "Health and Aged" and order the ones that interest you.

National Institute on Aging
NIA Information Center
Building 31, Room 5C27
31 Center Drive, MSC 2292
Bethesda, MD 20892
301-496-1752
www.nia.nih.gov

The NIA offers many free publications that can be ordered from the Public Information Office. Topics include: accidental hypothermia, aging and alcohol abuse, arthritis advice, cancer facts, exercise, foot care, flu, diabetes, high blood pressure, menopause, hospital hints, using medicines safely, prostrate, long term care, sexuality, smoking and more. They also conduct aging research and publish special reports and clinical summaries on a variety of subjects including health education, health promotion, disease prevention, nutrition, medications and safety.

U.S. Department of Labor
Employment & Training Administration Adult Training Programs
200 Constitution Ave., NW
Washington, DC 20210
877-889-5267
www.dol.gov/dol/topic/training/seniors.htm

This is an especially helpful service if you are looking for employment or job training. Currently, the Division of Older Workers offers the following programs:

1. As a result of the Older American Act, the "Part-Time Employment Program" was created for people over age 55. It provides jobs working in community services run by government agencies or nonprofit organizations.

2. Under the Job Training Partnership Act, all ages are eligible for job training services, however, 3 percent of those services (job training) and job placements must be for persons over the age of 55.

Administration on Aging (AOA)
1 Massachusetts Avenue
Washington, DC 20201
202-619-0724
www.aoa.gov

This umbrella organization functions to oversee all the state Departments on Aging and the Area Agencies on Aging offices around the United States.

The focus of these organizations is to provide help to mature adults.

Area Agency on Aging (AAA)

There are more than 700 Area Agencies on Aging that assist mature Americans throughout the United States, assuring such needed services as delivery of hot meals, chore services, energy assistance, adult day care, and transportation assistance. AAA coordinates services for older adults in specific geographic areas. It is an excellent resource for learning about programs for 65+ adults within a specific locale. AAAs are found by checking in the government pages of your telephone directory, or by contacting the State Office of Aging (see "State Agencies" below).

Department of Veterans Affairs
Washington, DC 20011
www.va.gov

The Department of Veterans Affairs can help veterans and their families with applications for educational assistance, life insurance, home loans and vocational rehabilitation. They also can help with securing medical care and dental benefits. And, as most of us know, they provide burial services to veterans and others who qualify. For information on what benefits and services you are eligible for as a result of serving your country contact: Department of Veteran Affairs, Office of Public Affairs, 810 Vermont Ave., NW, Washington, DC 20420. 800-827-1000.

State Agencies

State Offices on Aging—State Senior Discount Programs. This public organization, also referred to as the "State Unit on Aging," serves as the focal point for all matters relating to the needs of mature persons within a given state. Each state has an Office on Aging as do the District of Columbia and the U.S. territories. You can find your state Office on Aging from one of the following:

- One of the states areas Agencies on Aging.
- The Administration on Aging.
- The National Association of State Units on Aging.
- The Governor's Office.

Or contact the state office listed below. An example of some of the senior services and programs provided include: state senior discounts, senior passport programs, free hunting and fishing licenses, discounts on state park entrance fees and state camping facilities and long-term aging care, senior companions, brown bag, health care, adult day health care, and nutrition.

Alabama. Alabama Department of Senior Services, RSA Plaza, Suite 470, 770 Washington Ave., Montgomery, AL 36130-1851. 334-242-5743.

Alaska. Alaska Commission on Aging, Division of Senior and Disabilities Services, P.O. Box 110693, Juneau, AK 99811-0693. 907-465-3250.

Arizona. Aging and Adult Administration, Department of Economic Security, 1789 West Jefferson Street #950A, Phoenix, AZ 85007. 602-542-4446.

Arkansas. Division of Aging and Adult Services, Arkansas Dept. Of Human Services, P.O. Box 1437, Slot S-530, Little Rock, AR 72203-1437. 501-682-2441.

California. Department of Aging, 1300 National Dr., Suite 200, Sacramento, CA 95834. 916-419-7500.

Colorado. Division of Aging and Adult Services, Colorado Department of Human Services, 1575 Sherman Street, 10th Floor, Denver, CO 80203. 303-866-2800.

Connecticut. Aging Services Division, Department of Social Services, 25 Sigourney Street, 10th Floor, Hartford, CT 06106-5033. 860-424-5274.

Delaware. Division of Services for Aging and Adults with Physical Disabilities, Herman M. Holloway, Sr. Campus, Main Administration Building, 1901 N. Dupont Highway, New Castle, DE 19720. 302-453-3837.

District Of Columbia. Office of Aging, 441 Fourth Street NW, Suite 900S Washington, DC 20001. 202-724-5622.

Florida. Department of Elder Affairs, 4040 Esplanade Way, Tallahassee, FL 32399-7000. 850-414-2000.

Georgia. Division of Aging Services, Department of Human Resources, 2 Peachtree Street NW, Suite 9385, Atlanta, GA 30303. 404-657-5258.

Guam. Division of Senior Citizens, Department of Public Health and Social Services, P.O. Box 2816, Hagatna, Guam 96932. 011-671-735-7399.

Hawaii. Executive Office on Aging, 250 South Hotel Street, Room 406, Honolulu, HI 96813-2831. 808-586-0100.

Idaho. Idaho Commission on Aging, P.O. Box 83720, Boise, ID 83720-0007. 208-334-3833.

Illinois. Department on Aging, 421 East Capitol Avenue, Suite 100, Springfield, IL 62701-1789. 217-785-3356. Chicago Office: 312-814-2630. In-state toll free Senior HelpLine: 800-252-8966.

Indiana. Division of Aging, Family and Social Services Administration, 402 W. Washington Street, #W454, P.O. Box 7083, Indianapolis, IN 46207-7083. 317-232-7122.

Iowa. Iowa Department of Elder Affairs, Jessie M. Parker Building, 510 E. 12th Street, Suite 2, Des Moines, IA 50319. 515-725-3333.

Kansas. Department on Aging, New England Building, 503 S. Kansas Ave, Topeka, KS 66603-3404. 785-296-4986.

Kentucky. Division for Aging and Independent Living, 275 East Main Street, 3W-F, Frankfort, KY 40621. 502-564-6930.

Louisiana. Office of Elderly Affairs, P.O. Box 61, Baton Rouge, LA 70821-0061. 225-342-7100.

Maine. Office of Elder Services, Health and Human Services, 11 State House Station, 442 Civic Center Drive, Augusta, ME 04333. 207-287-9200.

Maryland. Department of Aging, 301 W. Preston St., Suite 1007, Baltimore, MD 21201. 410-767-1100.

Massachusetts. Massachusetts Executive Office of Elder Affairs, One Ashburton Place, 5th Floor, Boston, MA 02108. 617-727-7750.

Michigan. Office of Services to the Aging, P.O. Box 30676, Lansing, MI 48909-8176. 517-373-8230.

Minnesota. Board on Aging, P.O. Box 64976, St. Paul, MN 55164-0976. 651-431-2500.

Mississippi. Division on Aging and Adult Services, 750 N. State Street, Jackson, MS 39205. 601-359-4929.

Missouri. Department of Health and Senior Services, P.O. Box 570, Jefferson City, MO 65102. 573-751-6400.

Montana. Senior and Long Term Care Division, Department of Public Health & Human Services, 111

North Sanders, Room 211, Helena, MT 59620. 406-444-4077.

Nebraska. State Unit on Aging, Dept. of Health and Human Services, P.O. Box 95026, Lincoln, NE 68509-5044. 402-471-4623.

Nevada. Division for Aging Services, Department of Health and Human Services, 3416 Goni Road, Building D-132, Carson City, NV 89706. 775-687-4210.

New Hampshire. DHHS Bureau of Elderly and Adult Services, 129 Pleasant Street, Concord, NH 03301. 603-271-4680.

New Jersey. Department of Health and Senior Services, P.O. Box 360, Trenton, NJ 08625-0360. 609-292-7837; 800-367-6543.

New Mexico. Aging and Long-Term Services Department, Toney Anaya Building, 2550 Cerrillos Road, Santa Fe, NM 87505. 505-476-4799.

New York. State Office for the Aging, 2 Empire State Plaza, Albany, NY 12223-1251. 800-342-9871.

North Carolina. Division of Aging and Adult Services, 2101 Mail Service Center, Raleigh, NC 27699-2101. 919-733-3983.

North Dakota. Aging Services Division, Department of Human Services, 600 East Boulevard Avenue,

Dept. 325, Bismarck, ND 58505. 701-328-4601; 800-451-8693.

North Mariana Islands, CNMI Office on Aging, P.O. Box 2178, Commonwealth of the Northern Mariana Islands, Saipan, MP 96950. 670-233-1320/1321.

Ohio. Department on Aging, 50 West Broad Street, 9th Floor, Columbus, OH 42315. 614-466-6191.

Oklahoma. Aging Services Division, Department of Human Services, 2401 NW 23rd Street, Suite 40, Oklahoma City, OK 73107. 405-521-2281.

Oregon. Seniors and People with Disabilities, 500 Summer Street NE, E12, Salem, OR 97301-1073. 503-945-5921.

Pennsylvania. Department of Aging, Common-wealth of Pennsylvania, 555 Walnut Street, 5th Floor, Harrisburg, PA 17101-1919. 717-783-1550.

Puerto Rico. Governor's Office of Elderly Affairs, Commonwealth of Puerto Rico, Call Box 50063, Old San Juan Station, PR 00902. 787-721-5710; 787-721-4560.

Rhode Island. Department of Elderly Affairs, 35 Howard Avenue, Cranston, RI 02920. 401-462-4000.

American Samoa, Territorial Administration on Aging, Government of American Samoa, Pago Pago, American Samoa 96799. 011-684-633-1251.

South Carolina. Lieutenant Governor's Office on Aging, 1301 Gervais Street, Suite 200, Columbia, SC 29201. 803-734-9900.

South Dakota. Office of Adult Services and Aging, Richard F. Kneip Building, 700 Governors Drive, Pierre, SD 57501-2291. 605-773-3521.

Tennessee. Commission on Aging and Disability, Andrew Jackson Building, 8th Floor, 500 Deaderick Street, Nashville, TN 37243-0860. 615-741-2056.

Texas. Department of Aging and Disability Services, P.O. Box 149030, Austin, TX 78714-9030. 512-438-3011.

Utah. Division of Aging and Adult Services, Box 45500, 120 North 200 West, Room 325, Salt Lake City, UT 84103. 801-538-3910.

Vermont. Division of Disability and Aging Services, 30 Washington Street, Barre, VT 05641. 802-479-0531.

Virgin Islands. Virgin Islands Department of Human Services, Knud Hansen Complex, Building A, 1303 Hospital Ground, Charlotte Amalie, VI 00802. 340-774-0930.

Virginia. Department for the Aging, 1610 Forest Avenue, Suite 100, Richmond, VA 23229. 804-662-9333.

Washington. Aging and Disability Services Administration, Department of Social and Health Services, P.O. Box 45130, Olympia, WA 98504-5130. 360-725-2300.

West Virginia. West Virginia Bureau of Senior Services, 1900 Kanawha Boulevard East, Charleston, WV 25305. 304-558-3317.

Wisconsin. Bureau of Aging, Division of Community Services, One West Wilson Street, Room 450, P.O. Box 7851, Madison, WI 53707. 608-267-9880.

Wyoming. Division on Aging, Wyoming Department of Health, 6101 North Yellowstone Road, Suite 259B, Cheyenne, WY 82002-0710. 307-777-5340.

More Public Agencies

Catholic Charities Foster Grandparent Program
2625 Zanker Road, Suite 200
San Jose, CA 95134-2107
408-468-0100
www.ccsj.org

Coastline Elderly Services Foster Grandparent Program
1646 Purchase Street

New Bedford, MA 02740
508-999-6400
www.coastlineelderly.org
E-mail: information@CoastlineElderly.org

National Senior Service Corps (formerly ACTION)
1201 New York Ave., NW
Washington, DC 20525
202-606-5000
www.seniorcorps.org or www.nationalservice.org
The National Senior Service Corps is a national network of projects that place older volunteers in volunteer assignments in their communities. There are three umbrella programs. One is the Foster Grandparent Program, which links senior volunteers to children who need their help. Another is the Senior Companion Program, which places its volunteers with adults needing extra assistance. The third, the Retired and Senior Volunteer Program (RSVP) is "One stop shopping" for senior volunteers. Senior Corps Programs operate in local communities throughout the U.S. For a complete list of Foster Grandparent Agency Programs, call 202-606-5000.

U.S. Department of Health and Human Services
200 Independence Avenue, SW
Washington, D.C. 20201
202-619-0257; 877-696-6775
www.hhs.gov

Service Corps of Retired Executives (SCORE)
SCORE Association
409 3rd Street, SW, 6th Floor
Washington, DC 20024
800-634-0245
www.score.org
SCORE utilizes retired and semi-retired business-men to counsel new and existing small businesses. Volunteers are usually retired business professionals who want to share their expertise, experience and knowledge with the up and coming generation of business owners. Over 13,000 SCORE members volunteer nationwide. 703-487-3612; 800-634-0245.

U.S. Senate Special Committee on Aging
G31 Dirksen Senate Office Building
Washington, DC 20510-6400
202-224-5364
http://aging.senate.gov
The Senate Special Committee on aging is a great place to find out about existing, pending or anticipated legislation involving older adults. Send for free copies of special reports on a variety of topics from prescription drug price increases to women's health issues.

Private Organizations

American Association of Retired Persons (AARP)
Office of Communications
601 E St. NW, Washington, DC 20049
888-687-2277
www.aarp.org

AARP, the American Association of Retired Persons, is a nonprofit, nonpartisan organization dedicated to helping older Americans achieve lives of independence, dignity and purpose.

Founded in 1958, AARP is the nation's oldest and largest organization of older Americans, with a membership of more than 35 million. Membership is open to anyone age 50 or older, whether working or retired. AARP's motto is to "serve, not to be served." Membership dues (including spouse) are $12.50 for one year. AARP members receive *AARP The Magazine* bimonthly, and *AARP Bulletin* 11 times per year. *AARP The Magazine* has the second largest circulation of any U.S. magazine. The Association also distributes a wide range of specialized publications, many of which are available free of charge.

The Retired Teachers Division is open to former members of the National Retired Teachers Association and to soon-to-retire teachers, administrators, and other education professionals. Members receive the *NRTA Bulletin* and the NRTA edition of *AARP The Magazine*.

AARP priorities include four major areas that affect the quality of life that the AARP has targeted for a significant portion of its resources. These issue "initiatives" include: health care, women's issues, worker equity, and minority affairs. AARP represents a diverse population that includes workers and retirees, seniors re-entering the workforce, frail seniors over 80 living alone, people with comfortable standards of living, and those who struggle daily. A major AARP commitment is the development of legislative policy recommendations serving such a diverse group of older Americans.

AARP Member Services:

- AARP MarketPlace Program. Provides members with discounts on brand name products.
- Pharmacy Service. Provides prescription medicines and other health care items to members by mail or direct purchase.
- Travel Service. A wide variety of escorted or independent travel opportunities, i.e., tours, cruises, special-event programs and hosted living abroad programs, designed for AARP mature travelers.
- AARP Motoring Service. Includes a customized plan provided by GE Motor Club. Members of the AARP Motoring Plan receive 20 road service benefits.
- Group Health Insurance. Underwritten for AARP members by the United HealthCare Insurance Company.
- Auto/Homeowners Insurance. Offered by The Hartford Insurance Group to Association members.
- Mobile Home Insurance. Insurance for mobile home owners is provided by the Foremost Insurance Group.
- Educational Resources. AARP produces audiovisual program kits on issues ranging from health and nutrition, housing, and retirement planning to consumer protection and crime prevention. The kits are loaned free of charge to nonprofit organizations providing services to older people and members of the aging network.

The organization also publishes a continuing series of books of special usefulness and importance to middle-aged and older readers. Subjects include: money management, retirement planning, insurance decisions, foot care, crime prevention, widowhood, funeral planning, and housing alternatives.

AARP publications include more than 140 titles available free of charge upon request. These authoritative materials cover a variety of topics including health, consumer affairs, crime prevention, retirement planning, lifetime learning, and driver re-education. Information ranges from practical advice to "how-to" guides, demographics to resource publications. For a complete list of publications write: AARP Fulfillments, 601 E St. NW, Washington, DC 20049.

Community Services. More than 400,000 AARP volunteers are involved in community service programs nationwide that reinforce self-worth and self-reliance among older people. Through these programs, older Americans are given the opportunity to share their wisdom, experience, and abilities with those of all ages in need.

Some other beneficial programs administered by the AARP and its more than 3,700 local chapters and 2,500 Retired Teacher Association units throughout the United States include: Consumer Affairs Program, Criminal Justice Service, Mature Driving, Health Advocacy Services, Housing Program, Institute of Lifetime Learning, Intergenerational Program, International Activities, Inter-religious Liaison, Legal Counsel for the Elderly, National Gerontology Resource Center, National Retired Teachers Association Activities, Senior

Community Service Employment Program, Tax Aide Program, and Widowed Persons Service.

For a complete description of their services look up the web site at www.aarp.com.

National Senior Citizens Law Center
1101 14th St. NW, Suite 400
Washington, DC 20005
202-289-6976
www.nsclc.org

This is a legal services support center specializing in the legal problems of the elderly. It acts as an advocate on behalf of elderly and poor clients in legislative and administrative affairs. Contact them for copies of handbooks, testimonies and guides.

American Society on Aging
833 Market Street, Suite 511
San Francisco, CA 94103. 415-974-9600.
www.asaging.org
E-mail: info@asaging.org

Members include senior citizens, students, business persons, educators, researchers, administrators, health care and social service professionals who work to enhance the well being of older individuals and create unity among those working with and for the elderly. It focuses on the interests and needs of older people worldwide, particularly in the Third World. Besides offering continuing education programs on age-related issues, the American Society on Aging generates two important publications: *Generations*, a journal that provides practical current information in the field of aging, with emphasis on medical and social practice, research, and policy; and *Aging Today*, a bi-monthly newspaper that covers critical events and issues in the field of aging.

> National Council on Aging
> 1901 L Street NW, 4th Floor
> Washington, DC 20036
> 202-479-1200
> www.ncoa.org
> E-mail: info@ncoa.org

NCOA is the nation's first association of organizations dedicated to promoting the dignity, self-determination, well-being and contributions of older persons. Members help community organizations to enhance the lives of older adults, turn creative ideas into programs and services that help older people in hundreds of communities, and assume a national voice as a powerful advocate for public policies, societal attitudes, and business practices that promote vital aging. Offices are located in Cincinnati, OH, Ft. Lauderdale, FL, Hempstead, NY, Los Angeles, CA, Bangor, ME, Trenton, NJ, New York City, NY, San Francisco, CA, San Jose, CA, and West Palm Beach, FL.

This group also promotes and provides resources for ministries with older adults. NICA works with more than 25 Protestant, Jewish, Catholic, and orthodox organizations to provide training and develop resources through local congregations and religious organizations. They approach senior issues by representing the spiritual concerns of older Americans in public and private forums. Membership is $47.50 annually.

Catholic Golden Age
Box 249
Olyphant, PA 18447
800-836-5699
www.catholicgoldenage.org

A nonprofit association of senior citizens founded in 1975, Catholic Golden Age provides spiritual benefits as well as material benefits and discounts to men and women age 50 and over. Currently Catholic Golden Age has over 400,000 members. For updated discounts check the web site: www.catholicgoldenage.org

Jewish Association for Services for the Aged (JASA)
132 West 31st St.
New York, NY 10001
212-273-5272
www.jasa.org

Established on the East Coast in 1968, this social welfare organization provides the services necessary to enable older adults to remain in the community. There are over 60,000 members, served in New York City and Nassau and Suffolk counties. Services include: information and referral to appropriate health, welfare, educational, social, recreational, and vacation services, government benefits and entitlements; personal counseling; financial assistance; health and medical service counseling; counseling on housing and long-term care; homemaker service; group educational and recreational activities; hot lunch programs; referral to summer camps; legal services; protective services; reaching out to the isolated; and programs for the independent senior clubs.

National Active and Retired Federal Employees Association (NARFE)
606 North Washington Street
Alexandria, VA 22314-1914
703-838-7760
www.narfe.org

This is an association of federal retirees and their families. They represent an aggressive lobbying force on Capitol Hill whose purpose is to protect retirement benefits. Membership includes an annual subscription to *NARFE Magazine*, and membership in a local chapter. Other NARFE benefits include:

- Discounts on Avis, Dollar and Alamo car rentals.
- Travel packages, group tours, and discounts.
- Moving services.
- NARFE MasterCard with no annual fee for six months.
- Emergency services.
- Health, life, dental, auto, and long-term care insurance plans.

National Older Women's League (OWL)
3300 North Fairfax Drive, Suite 218
Arlington, VA 22201
703-812-7990 or 800-825-3695.
www.owl-national.org

In this country, the problems of aging are largely women's problems. More than 70 percent of the nearly 4 million persons over 65 living in poverty are women. Fewer than 20 percent of older women currently receive any pension income. Most women over 65 depend on Social

Security as their only significant income. Millions of mid-life women have no health insurance.

The Older Women's League works to change these facts. It is the first grassroots membership organization to focus exclusively on women as they age. OWL works to provide mutual support for its members, helps them achieve economic and social equity, and works to improve the image and status of older women. It provides educational materials, training for citizen advocates, and informational publications dealing with the important issues facing women as they grow older. Members are eligible for supplemental insurance plans and receive discounts on all OWL publications. Washington location: 2034B 17th St. NW, Washington, DC 20009. 202-588-1734.

American Legion
P.O. Box 1055
Indianapolis, IN 46206
317-630-1200
www.legion.org

The American Legion is the nation's largest veterans organization. While it isn't made up solely of those 50+, it does include a large group of older veterans. *American Legion Magazine*, for example, has a circulation of more than 2.5 million. Its average reader is 60 years old. The Legion's most visible activity is its work on behalf of veterans, their survivors, and dependents. In addition, a large portion of the American Legion's resources are channeled into education programs and citizenship activities for youths. Each year more than 200 American Legion community service projects costing more than $5 million in aid touch the lives of millions of Americans.

Note: Service organizations such as the American Legion, Rotary, Lions, Kiwanis, and Elks also have large age 50+ constituencies. These groups also have both local and regional clubs.

National Caucus and Center on the Black Aged
1220 L St., NW, Suite 800
Washington, DC 20005
202-637-8400
www.ncba-aged.org

This organization seeks to improve living conditions for low-income elderly Black Americans. They advocate changes in federal and state laws by improving the economic, health, and social status of low-income senior citizens. They also promote community awareness of problems and issues affecting this group. It operates an employment program involving older persons in 14 states and sponsors, owns, and manages rental housing for the elderly.

National Hispanic Council on Aging
734 15th St., NW, Suite 1050
Washington, DC 20005
202-347-9733
www.nhcoa.org

Members of this organization work for the well-being of the Hispanic elderly through research, policy analysis, and projects, and provide a network for organizations and community groups interested in the Hispanic elderly.

National Association for Hispanic Elderly
The Association Nacional Pro Personas Mayores
234 East Colorado Blvd., Suite 300
Pasadena, CA 91101
626-564-1988
www.anppm.org
This organization focuses on helping rural elderly in southern Texas and northern California to gain access to supportive services offered under the Older Americans Act. Trained volunteers help the elderly obtain needed assistance and local services.

National Indian Council on Aging
10501 Montgomery Blvd. N.E., Suite 210
Albuquerque, NM 87111
505-292-2001
www.nicoa.org
This organization seeks to bring about improved, comprehensive services to the Indian and Alaskan native elderly. It acts as a focal point for the articulation of the needs of the Indian elderly, disseminates information on Indian aging programs, provides technical assistance and training opportunities to tribal organizations, and conducts research on the needs of Indian elderly.

National Pacific/Asian Resource Center
1511 3rd Avenue, Suite 914
Seattle, WA 98101-1626
206-624-1221 or 800-336-2722
www.napca.org

This group's goals are to ensure and improve the delivery of health and social services to elderly Pacific/ Asians and increase the availability of community-based services to the elderly. They also produce several informative publications and a national community service directory.

National Committee to Preserve Social Security and Medicare (NCPSSM)
10 G Street, N.E., Suite 600
Washington, DC 20002
202-216-0420
www.ncpssm.org
The NCPSSM is a highly vocal organization and one of the largest lobbying groups in America dealing with Social Security, Medicare, and other senior issues on Capitol Hill.

60 Plus Association
1600 Wilson Blvd., Suite 960
Arlington, VA 22209
888-560-7587
www.60plus.org
This national lobbying organization is targeted to a politically conservative audience. There are more than 2 million members working to promote the advancement of senior Americans through sound fiscal policy. Their purpose is to inform the American public of the needs of senior citizens and of the programs and policies being carried out by the government and other groups. Members' benefits include a health insurance plan; discounted health benefits; newsletters; and discounts

on lodging, car rentals, magazines, and movie theaters. Dues are $25 a year.

Military Officers Association of America (MOAA)
201 N. Washington St.
Alexandria, VA 22314-2529
800-234-6622
www.moaa.org

This association is an independent nonprofit organization dedicated to maintaining a strong national defense and preserving the entitlements and benefits of uniformed services personnel, their families, and survivors. MOAA is the largest military officers, association in the country. Members receive *Military Officer* magazine, containing reports on Congress and matters of special interest. Other benefits include counseling in employment assistance, personal affairs, dependent scholarship loans/grants, survivor assistance, and retirement information. There are also discounts on car rentals, a discount travel program, health screenings, sports holidays, a mail-order prescription program, group health and life insurance plans, financial services, and an extended car warranty program.

Spry Foundation
3916 Rosemary Street
Chevy Chase, MD 20815
301-656-3405
www.spry.org
E-mail: morganr@spry.org

SPRY helps older adults plan for a healthy and financially secure future.

Canadian Association of Retired Persons (C.A.R.P.)
Fifty-Plus.net, Suite 300
27 Queen Street East
Toronto, Ontario M5C 2M6 Canada
416-363-7063
www.fifty-plus.net

This organization is a national nonprofit, nonpolitical association of Canadians over 50 established to promote the interests of mature Canadians. Membership is $19.95 a year (including spouse). This group is the Canadian counterpart to the AARP, and has over 375,000 members. Benefits include *Carp* Magazine, discounts on health care, home and car insurance, car rentals, hotels, theaters, and travel.

Books Available from Santa Monica Press

www.santamonicapress.com • 1-800-784-9553

The Bad Driver's Handbook
*Hundreds of Simple Maneuvers
to Frustrate, Annoy, and
Endanger Those Around You*
by Zack Arnstein and
Larry Arnstein
192 pages $12.95

Calculated Risk
*The Extraordinary Life of
Jimmy Doolittle*
by Jonna Doolittle Hoppes
360 pages $24.95

Captured!
*Inside the World of Celebrity
Trials*
by Mona Shafer Edwards
176 pages $24.95

Creepy Crawls
A Horror Fiend's Travel Guide
by Leon Marcelo
384 pages $16.95

**Educating the Net
Generation**
*How to Engage Students in the
21st Century*
by Bob Pletka, Ed.D.
192 pages $16.95

**The Encyclopedia of
Sixties Cool**
*A Celebration of the Grooviest
People, Events, and Artifacts of
the 1960s*
by Chris Strodder
336 pages $24.95

**Exotic Travel Destinations
for Families**
by Jennifer M. Nichols and
Bill Nichols
360 pages $16.95

Footsteps in the Fog
Alfred Hitchcock's San Francisco
by Jeff Kraft and
Aaron Leventhal
240 pages $24.95

French for Le Snob
*Adding Panache to Your
Everyday Conversations*
by Yvette Reche
400 pages $16.95

Haunted Hikes
*Spine-Tingling Tales and Trails
from North America's National
Parks*
by Andrea Lankford
376 pages $16.95

How to Speak Shakespeare
by Cal Pritner and
Louis Colaianni
144 pages $16.95

**How to Win Lotteries,
Sweepstakes, and Contests
in the 21st Century**
by Steve Ledoux
240 pages $14.95

James Dean Died Here
*The Locations of America's
Pop Culture Landmarks*
by Chris Epting
312 pages $16.95

L.A. Noir
The City as Character
by Alain Silver and
James Ursini
176 pages $19.95

Led Zeppelin Crashed Here
*The Rock and Roll Landmarks
of North America*
by Chris Epting
336 pages $16.95

Letter Writing Made Easy!
*Featuring Sample Letters for
Hundreds of Common Occasions*
by Margaret McCarthy
208 pages $12.95

Movie Star Homes
by Judy Artunian and
Mike Oldham
312 pages $16.95

Redneck Haiku
Double-Wide Edition
by Mary K. Witte
240 pages $11.95

**Route 66 Adventure
Handbook**
by Drew Knowles
312 pages $16.95

**The Ruby Slippers,
Madonna's Bra, and
Einstein's Brain**
*The Locations of America's
Pop Culture Artifacts*
by Chris Epting
312 pages $16.95

**Rudolph, Frosty, and Captain
Kangaroo**
*The Musical Life of Hecky
Krasnow—Producer of the World's
Most Beloved Children's Songs*
by Judy Gail Krasnow
424 pages $24.95

School Sense
*How to Help Your Child Succeed
in Elementary School*
by Tiffani Chin, Ph.D.
408 pages $16.95

The Shakespeare Diaries
A Fictional Autobiography
by J.P. Wearing
456 pages $27.95

Silent Traces
*Discovering Early Hollywood
Through the Films of Charlie
Chaplin*
by John Bengtson
304 pages $24.95

The Sixties
Photographs by Robert Altman
192 pages $39.95

Tiki Road Trip
*A Guide to Tiki Culture in North
America*
2nd Edition
by James Teitelbaum
360 pages $16.95

Tower Stories
An Oral History of 9/11
by Damon DiMarco
528 pages $27.95

**The Ultimate Counterterrorist
Home Companion**
*Six Incapacitating Holds
Involving a Spatula and Other
Ways to Protect Your Family*
by Zack Arnstein and
Larry Arnstein
168 pages $12.95